# Up All Night

# UpAll Night

*Practical Wisdom from Mothers and Fathers*

**Edited by Gregory Orfalea
and Barbara Rosewicz**

**Foreword by Alice McDermott**

Paulist Press
New York/Mahwah, N.J.

*Cover and book design by Sharyn Banks*

Library of Congress Cataloging-in-Publication Data

Up all night : practical wisdom from mothers and fathers / edited by Gregory Orfalea and Barbara Rosewicz ; foreword by Alice McDermott.
    p. cm.
  ISBN 0-8091-4235-X (alk. paper)
  1. Parenting—Religious aspects—Christianity. 2. Child rearing—Religious aspects—Christianity. I. Orfalea, Gregory, 1949–
II. Rosewicz, Barbara.

  BV4529. U6 2004
  248.8'45—dc22

                                                          2004001635

Published by Paulist Press
997 Macarthur Boulevard
Mahwah, New Jersey 07430

www.paulistpress.com

Printed and bound in the
United States of America

*For Eileen and Jerry,*
*and six wonderful boys—*
*Matthew, Andrew, and Luke Orfalea*
*and Joseph, Jacob, and Luke Seib—*
*and for the remarkable Blessed Sacrament community*

# Contents

# Foreword

## *Alice McDermott*

The biological imperative cannot be denied: nature provides the human parent with a depth of emotion commensurate with our offspring's initial and prolonged helplessness. Were it not so, there would be little hope for our species. Let's face it: even among mammals, we human babies are incredible wimps—mewlers and pukers at birth (as Shakespeare might have put it), and whining schoolboys creeping toward self-sufficiency for a good many years after. Given our frail beginnings, it seems clear that the need for a watchful adult for every human child is not merely a Dickensian conceit or a Disneyesque fantasy, but an indisputable fact of nature, a biological imperative, a matter of life or death. Someone must care for the human newborn, toddler, child, and more often than not, that someone is a parent. That the ferociousness of the child's need is quite often met by an equal ferociousness of emotion on the part of the parent is, no doubt, one way nature insures the continuation of our race.

And yet the parents whose testimonials are collected here see in their love for their children something more than wily nature at work. If there is one recurrent theme throughout these forty-four essays, it is this: that the unconditional love these mothers and fathers feel for their children is nothing less than a reflection of the Divine Love. Is it religious hyperbole? Catholic delusion? A spiritual sugar coating for what is merely a biological necessity? The experiences recounted here prove otherwise.

For if the emotional transformation that takes place in the hearts of mothers and fathers at the birth of a child can easily be attributed to hormone and circumstance and need, how then to account for the persistence of that emotion once the hormones and the circumstances and the needs have changed? How to account for the persistence of that love, as recounted in these pages, through the exhausting routines of childhood, the challenges of adolescence, the achievement of a child's full maturity as an adult? How to account for the persistence of that love, the consistency of its nature and its strength, when it is for a stepchild, an adopted child, an irreparably damaged child, or a child who has died? The argument for biology and practicality and the simple preservation of the species grows thin. Something more is at work here, as these parents have discovered. More than eye has seen or ear has heard. A glimpse, a reflection, as they hold their children in their arms, of the love the Creator has for us.

In my own biography as a parent, my return to the life of a practicing Catholic no doubt was inspired by the births of my children. There were practical incentives: a ready-made community, access to good schools, a routine of ritual and celebration that gave me opportunity to show off my darlings in their best clothes. There was, too, the opportunity to pause in the midst of the hectic routine, a chance to form into formal prayer the minute-by-minute petitions to On High that is the mother's lot (let him/her not fall, not cry, not fail, not forget, make the bus, make the basket, sit still, get up, get in, be well, be happy). There was also a chance to be reminded each week, too, of the power of parable, the possibility of forgiveness, the miracle of hope—useful benefits all for a busy parent, but, as with the biological imperative, insufficient alone to describe the depth of my experience. For it was not merely the perceived benefit of religious structure that brought me back to church with my children. It was, at heart, the new appreciation their births had given me for creation itself, for God as Father and Mother, for love as the First Cause.

As the parents whose voices are collected here will prove, no one who has raised children will argue against practicality. Amidst the testimonies to Divine Love you will find plenty of wisdom regarding how to cope, how to get through it, what to brace yourself for, and what you'll never see coming. The practical benefits of the biological imperative—from the mechanisms that let down a mother's milk to the ones that wake a father in the middle of the night when a certain teenager is not yet home—are not to be discounted. But what these voices—eloquent, hesitant, poetic, straightforward, earnest, wry—also confirm is the belief that our children's need does not shape our love for them, rather that Love has shaped their need. That nature has as its purpose something more than the preservation of the species. That through the astonishing emotion we feel for our children our

Creator seeks to share with us his joy, his pride, his own astonishing love.

Up all night, indeed; these parents understand the experience. Up all night in humility (and worry), in gratitude (and exhaustion), in contentment (and expectation), in love, in awe.

*Alice McDermott, who teaches at Johns Hopkins University, is the National Book Award-winning author of the novel* Charming Billy. *Her latest novel is* Child of My Heart. *She and her husband David Armsrong have three sons: Will, Eames, and Patrick.*

# Introduction

*Father Percival D'Silva*

Is there any vocation more difficult than raising a family? I doubt it. The twenty-two mothers and twenty-two fathers here have "been there." They are still there. They know what it is like. The experience has taught them, shaken them, hurt them, matured them, grayed them, enriched them, and finally sanctified them. Hence this book, *Up All Night: Practical Wisdom from Mothers and Fathers*.

This book has an unusual history. Since 1989, mothers and fathers from the Shrine of the Most Blessed Sacrament in Washington, D.C., have been speaking at the Masses on Mother's Day and Father's Day. We priests have turned over the microphone to those living that life every day. The result has been amazing, and that tradition is the source of these essays, culled from more than one hundred talks.

Though the tradition is unique to my knowledge, the people aren't. They are ordinary people, raising ordinary children, in a normal, ordinary way. But they are doing it with such extraordinary ordinariness!

I am a Catholic priest, but I was born and raised in Bombay, India, where the vast majority of people are Hindu and the rest mostly Muslim. I believe that though most of the pieces here are by Catholics, the lessons about parenting in this most difficult and selfish age can speak to anyone, be they Christian, Jewish, Hindu, Muslim, or even to those outside any established religion. There is "God within Us" here, to be sure. That God requires the same virtues of parents of all faiths—and those with none—and gives them the same trials. Where there is a good parent, there is God, whether that parent realizes it or not.

You will find much of St. Paul's "clothing" here: "Clothe yourselves with compassion, kindness, humility, meekness, and patience. Bear with one another and, if anyone has a complaint against another, forgive each other; just as the Lord has forgiven you, so you also must forgive. Above all, clothe yourselves with love, which binds everything together in perfect harmony" (Col 3:12–14).

In a society in which children seem not to be valued except as markets for commodities, we should heed the words of Pope John Paul II: "Children are the springtime of a family and society.... Children are...the hope that continually blossoms, a project that starts ever new, a future that opens without ceasing. They present the flowering of married love, which is found and strengthened in them" (Third World Meeting of Families, October 14, 2000).

In a very real way, families "create" church at home. The U.S. Conference of Bishops has told us, "The profound and ordinary moments of daily life—meal times, work days, vacations, expressions of love and intimacy, household chores, caring for a sick child or elderly parents, and even conflicts over things like how to celebrate holidays, discipline children, or spend money—all are the threads from which you can weave a pattern of holiness." The bishops don't mince words when it comes to the importance of family, quoting John Paul II: "The future of humanity passes by way of the family" (*Familiaris Consortio,* #86).

We have all sorts of experts telling us how to do this precious thing called parenting. Psychologists. Counselors. Professors. Rabbis. Priests! But when do we hear from the parents themselves? Rarely.

The pieces in *Up All Night* offer practical wisdom "from the trenches." The "how-to" here is not out of the blue but is the result of years, sometimes decades, of experience, which is often fraught with difficulty, pain, and loss. And yet there is such beauty here! And such humor! A reader will find, I am convinced, the path to a happy, fruitful, and successful family life in these pages.

Notice I did not say the word *easy.* There is no easy family life. But I am convinced the home must be a shrine. The key players in this sanctuary are the mother and father. In a real way, they are the priests of the home. If anyone is to take their children to God, it is they. In some ways, it is a fearful burden. Parents can make or break their children. But however hard, this burden can lead to happiness and fulfillment.

From most homes children walk out into the world. If well-prepared, they will walk out as saints-in-the-making, ready to rear their own young. If not, society is the loser.

My sincere prayer and hope is that those who read this book will derive the inspiration and guidance that I have, as well as the families and young people who have heard these words over the years. Now we have captured them for others.

I am deeply indebted to Barbara Rosewicz and Gregory Orfalea, the editors. Their help, expertise, and dedication beggar description.

# Soon, Very Soon

*Patrick A. Malone*

When our youngest son Brendan was three, he gradually began to lose the gift of speech. Eventually Brendan became mute, and at the same time he developed other behaviors—clapping his hands, running aimlessly, chewing on himself, and suddenly bursting into uncontrolled sobbing or giggling. Finally we were told that Brendan had autism, a severe case of it. This was a little boy who knew his alphabet at eighteen months and spent hours looking at books.

For a time we pursued all sorts of therapies and cures. We even took him to Lourdes in France. But nothing seemed to help. We spent a long time grieving about the little boy we lost. Now we have reconciled ourselves to raising a severely handicapped son who will need lifelong special care. It is still painful to see a youngster chatting happily with his father at a McDonald's or on a subway train. I still have intense dreams in which suddenly Brendan begins talking normally as if he had never stopped.

Sometimes it is hard to watch normal children playing with each other, because Brendan has no relationship with other children and cannot really play. They say that one of the striking features of autism is an inability to engage in imaginative play.

Brendan spends most of his time alone with himself. That seems to be his preference. However, he can be quite affectionate, and for that we are very grateful. He can communicate emotion very well, and he can understand others' emotions. When voices are raised in our house, as sometimes happens, Brendan gets upset. He reminds us of our need to calm down and get along and love each other.

Brendan's older brothers, Ian and Chris, are both very good with him. Chris has even spent summers working in Brendan's classroom with other autistic children. My wife Vicki is also wonderful with Brendan, who requires a lot of patience. He's always pulling up plants or making a mess with food or dirtying his pants. Brendan has brought all of us closer together in a mysterious way.

What do you do with a little boy who is an eternal toddler? Once, years ago, when one of our older boys did something charming at age two or three, I remember thinking, *Wouldn't it be great if he never grew up, if he were always this innocent and wonderful?* I remembered that thought when a doctor at Johns Hopkins told us, after examining Brendan, that he was functioning at a two-year-old level and may continue to do so. When that happened, something allowed me to cough up a bitter thought: *Be careful what you wish for, because it might come true.* But I set it aside and moved on.

What can a parent do with a child like Brendan? Well, as with any two-year-old, you tickle him and play peekaboo. You read him books. You play horsey. You try to make him laugh. And when he does laugh, when he throws his arms around you and sighs with joy, you know that life is sweet. It doesn't matter that he can't tell you he's happy because you can see it and feel it.

It's important to adjust your expectations, too. When Brendan was first diagnosed, we thought, well, he'll just be a little delayed in school, but maybe he'll catch up by the third or fourth grade. As his silence deepened, we realized he might never go to professional school or college. But could he do something, someday, to make a contribution?

Now we think that some kind of sheltered work might be the most we can hope for with Brendan. But does it really matter? He doesn't need to earn his place. He did that when God set him down in our midst. What counts is that he is secure and comfortable and safe, and as happy as we can manage.

Simple things count the most with a boy like Brendan. SAT scores don't matter. A really good hot dog slathered in ketchup is the thing he enjoys, or a chocolate shake at the end of a ride on our tandem bike. That's living!

Brendan inherited from his parents our love of good eating. Thus, he has no handicap whatsoever in locating and devouring any sweet we have tried to squirrel away for some later time. He seems to be saying, "Let tomorrow take care of itself! Let's live today!" And his face glows with the biggest smile you've ever seen.

Brendan has taught me to take pleasure in the simplest things, to let go of petty grievances, to live for the day. We do worry, of course, about tomorrow. That is the job of parents. What will happen to Brendan when we are gone? And we have other issues of more immediate concern: What will happen if his stormy moods worsen? He chews on his arm sometimes when he is frustrated or when he just needs some stimulation. Even now, pre-puberty, he likes to reach down into his pants and pull on himself. What will it be like in a few years when his child's mind will inhabit an adult's body?

As parents of an autistic child, we have a thousand questions like these. Brendan's therapists listen and nod with sympathy. Words come out of their mouths, but we learned long ago that they don't know the answers either. Parents have to look somewhere else for answers.

Thus, at the same time we were learning to adjust to Brendan's disability, I began a spiritual journey to understand and deal with this tragedy. For a time I was angry with God. We were good Catholics, so I thought. How could we deserve this? How could a fate so cruel befall a little boy, especially one who seemed so innocent and lovable? When I stood at the shrine at Lourdes, I asked for answers to these questions or for some kind of sign. Better yet, I wanted a miracle that would have Brendan speaking again as if he'd never stopped, just as in my dreams.

No voice answered me, and no miracle happened. I did, however, gradually find some measure of peace and calm dealing with the difficulties that naturally accompany our very special boy.

Some well-meaning people have told us that God doesn't deal out challenges that we can't handle. I would like to believe that, but I'm not always so sure. What about those people who seem crushed by adversity? Did they just not pray enough?

I have puzzled many times over the words from the gospel that speak of fathers and sons. In Luke's Gospel, Jesus says,

> "So I say to you, Ask, and it will be given to you; search, and you will find; knock, and the door will be opened for you. For everyone who asks receives, and everyone who searches finds, and for everyone who knocks, the door will be opened. Is there anyone among you who, if your child asks for a fish, will give a snake instead of a fish? Or if the child asks for an egg, will give a scorpion? If you then, who are evil, know how to give good gifts to your children, how much more will the heavenly Father give the Holy Spirit to those who ask him!" (Luke 11:9–13)

Thus I have prayed many times to God: "Ok, I'm asking, God. I'm seeking, Lord. I'm knocking on your door. Open up, Lord. Let the little boy talk. Remove these unclean spirits that tie his tongue."

And as I have looked around me, I see other parents struggling to help their children who have cancer or cerebral palsy, or less devastating problems. Their faith can be severely tested, too.

A great river of suffering flows through life on earth. What does it all mean?

When we were kids and took family trips, we sat in the backseat of the family car and asked over and over, "When are we gonna get there, Daddy?" Dad always replied, "Soon."

I think God sees us that way and He also responds, "Soon." But God's time and my time are not the same, just as a parent's time and a child's time are not the same.

Jesus climbed up on the cross to show us the way. Even he despaired, asking "My God, my God, why have you forsaken me?" (Matt 27:46).

Suffering is a necessary part of life, but after suffering there is life eternal. That is God's promise. That is our firm belief.

And so we take up our crosses, we fathers with children, and we struggle through. We stumble and despair, but we smile and we keep going, because we know, through Christ's suffering and resurrection, that there is a promise and a hope.

It may not happen in this life. But by God's measure of time, it will happen soon, very soon.

*Patrick A. Malone is a lawyer in Washington, D.C., who represents injured people in medical malpractice and product liability suits. His wife Vicki is a personal chef and homemaker. Their three children are Ian, Chris, and Brendan.*

# A Thing Worth Doing Badly

*John Mueller*

For someone my age to speak about being a father is like hearing a book report from someone who's only a third of the way through the book. I need to start with *my* father, because his life is a book I did read to the end. He died of cancer in 1998, and a year before that, I videotaped a long interview about his life that I've recently been editing for the family.

I grew up thinking that it's normal to be one of twelve children (I was the sixth), that everything naturally runs smoothly in such a household—good neighborhoods, mostly Catholic grade schools, all twelve going to college—it all just happens. That colossal illusion, I now see, was in large part my father's doing. He was not only the oldest of eight. In 1941, he was pulled out of line in Navy boot camp, based on his test scores, and ordered to help organize and run several schools that trained hundreds of radio technicians every month for four years. After the war he ran the engineering department of a large corporation that designed and sold vending machines.

Though skilled at organizing people, what he really liked was tackling problems no one else had solved. He had infinite patience with an appliance that didn't work, though not with a child who didn't work. But sometimes his wry humor got the better of Navy discipline. My mother recalls a time she found the noise unbearable as she tried to fix dinner; she marched into the living room only to find my father reclining in his easy chair, placidly surveying the sources of commotion. "Richard!" she said. "How can you just sit there in the middle of all this?" "Aleatha," he replied, "where else can you get so much cheap entertainment?"

I think each of us twelve had the secret fantasy of being an only child, which somehow coexisted with the secret conviction that he or she was the "special one" of the family. When I asked how this trick was done, my father said he tried to make sure that each of us excelled at something besides schoolwork (that was expected). My next older brother, Paul, was an amateur radio operator. My youngest brother, Jim, sailed a Sunfish in sailboat races. Today, Jim and his wife live on an oceangoing sailboat and keep in touch with land through Paul by radio. My father taught others to fish, to camp, to shoot, to craft, to wire, and to build. Once he even got my mother up on water skis.

My mother never knew her real father, and it affected her whole life. By marrying my father, she gained a large network of German Catholic relatives and a new faith—faith in a heavenly, never-wavering father to replace the earthly one who had left and the wavering father her husband sometimes was. In later years, my parents' marriage was not always a happy one. But you can't judge a marriage by a snapshot. My father eventually returned to the Church, fulfilling my mother's long-term prayers. Then, during his extended struggle with cancer, his impatience burned off, revealing a basic sweetness. It even rekindled their romance. My father arranged everything, not just to provide for my mother after he was gone, but to show her, with the outward affection she'd always craved, that she was the most important person in his life. He remained a father to the end, showing us how you can die with faith and humor.

To some extent, we learn by observing our parents and following their example; to some extent, we learn by observing and avoiding their mistakes. I've learned that it's never too late to show your wife you love her—but on the other hand, it's never too early. I've learned that love is not just a feeling, so that if the feeling fades, so must the love. It's closer to the truth to say that feelings follow love, which is there even or especially when the feelings aren't.

I also learned that faith in God and faithfulness to your spouse are connected: in each case, you need to displace yourself from the center of the universe. My parents' shared Catholic faith was the foundation of their marriage; it also contained the seeds of its re-flowering.

My own situation is more complicated: Linda is a Methodist, whereas I returned to the Catholic Church after we were married. It's been helpful for me to know that Linda and I share not just matrimony, but also baptism. According to the Church, marriage is a sacrament for any two baptized Christians. The one thing I remember from college sociology is that groups with an even number of people are more likely to break up than groups with an odd number—because a group without a majority is more likely to reach stalemate. If you believe marriage is the joining of not two but three people—you, your wife, and Christ—there's always a working majority. For some reason, he seems to vote an awful lot with Linda.

Linda's and my roles are similar to what they were for Linda's parents, but almost the reverse of my parents': on most day-to-day matters, Linda is the organizer and I'm an organizee. Besides running the household and reviewing books for a newspaper, Linda can run a book sale or be room mother, lunch mother, soccer team manager, or Home and School secretary with equal ease. Despite years of practice helping at Cub Scouts and basketball clinics, my administrative skills are overtaxed by having to pick five ten-year-old girls to substitute in a CYO summer basketball game.

It used to bother me that Linda can be the kind of mother her mother was, but I'm not the kind of father my father was. It has helped me to realize that being a father is a thing worth doing badly. There are some things in life, G. K. Chesterton observed, that we wish to see done well if they are done at all. He specifically mentioned playing the church organ, and we can add things like open-heart surgery, piloting an airliner, or singing the National Anthem on television. But the most basic human things, Chesterton said, a person must do for himself, even if he does them badly: things like writing a love letter, blowing your nose, or voting.

Being a father is decidedly a thing worth doing badly when the alternative is not to do it at all. If being a father is merely a thing worth doing well, what happens on the day you realize you're not a very good father? The obvious temptation is to stop being a father. But if being a father is a thing worth doing badly, then that's the day you can start being a father.

Of course, our Lord assures us that being a father is not rocket science: "Is there anyone among you who, if your child asks for bread, will give a stone? Or if the child asks for a fish, will give a snake?" As a ten-year-old might say, "Well, duh!" In some ways, it's harder to be a son or daughter than to be a father. Deep down, children believe, even when they rebel, that the parent is right. They count on it. This terrible trust can be damaging when the parent finds it difficult, as I do, to admit being wrong. Fortunately in this case a wife is always willing to help.

It's also fortunate that children are not merely what we make of them. What I like most about my kids, even more than the ways in which they resemble their parents, is the ways in which they are different. Our son Christian is a talented artist, good with words, and he has a zany and subversive sense of humor; and along with the responsibility of being the oldest, he has learned to be a Pied Piper for children, a trait which will serve him well as a father. Peter, besides being musical and possessing encyclopedic knowledge of the Civil War, is, like his namesake St. Peter, mercurial and generous to a fault; he aspires to great things for his faith. As for Lucy, the world is her oyster. She's outgoing—a trait that must skip generations—and actively seeks to draw newcomers and outsiders into the circle. Also, she applies herself to learn the things a girl needs to know: like how, as the only girl on her Little League team, to knock in two runs, with two outs and the bases loaded.

With this cast of characters, I'm interested to see what happens next and how the book turns out. Probably, thirty or forty years from now, when Christian or Peter or Lucy interviews me through my hearing aid, I'll be as clueless as I am today. But I suspect I'll be able to say what my father said—and it was the closest I ever heard him come to a boast: "When you look at all these great kids, you say to yourself, 'Well, I must have done something right.'"

*John Mueller is chief economist of a financial markets firm in Chevy Chase, Maryland. He and his wife, the writer Linda Mallon, have three children: Christian, Peter, and Lucy.*

# The Chance to Hear "Look at Me!"

*Timothy Shriver*

Stories of faith are not always stories of comfort. Probably the two most famous father stories in our Christian culture offer particularly difficult and painful tales of a father's love: the story of Abraham and Isaac, and the story of Jesus in the Garden of Gethsemane.

Think about Abraham and Isaac, the terrifying scene of the slow walk of father and son up the side of the mountain, the intimacy of the two, and then the haunting words of the boy: "Father, where is the animal?"

And think of Jesus on that last night, literally sweating blood, abandoned by friends, and then turning to his abba, his daddy, and begging that the cup might pass.

In both cases, the father takes his son to the point of agony: Abraham ties his son and prepares to make of him a sacrifice, and God the Father answers the cry of his only Son with a trip to Jerusalem—where awaits physical torture and the butchery of the cross.

These are tough images of what it means to be a father.

My life with my father and as a father is much more pedestrian than all of this. My memories of my childhood and my father are full of excitement and anticipation. I remember our Saturday mornings, when my dad would stay home and wake me up early so that we could go off to Mass, to the 7-Eleven, and to the car wash. And I remember running by him one afternoon and hearing him say to his friends, "Look at Timmy go. Look how fast he is!" I remember his taking me on a trip, all the way to Alaska at the age of six— just the two of us. And I remember riding my bike for the first time as he pushed me off, and I screamed, "Look at me! Look at me!"

These are my stories of special times, the times when I knew and felt that my dad and I had something special. The challenge of fatherhood is to remember the extraordinary chance we have as fathers to do something special with our children, however simple, and to listen to them as they burst out with the joy-filled call, "Look at me!" I'm not sure there is anything more important we can do than that.

Now times have changed since I was a child of four or six or eight. Men are supposed to listen more and lead less, care more and demand less, offer more and structure less. So many of us with young children can get caught in a web of analysis about our new and changed roles.

But change notwithstanding, I'm sure that every father, at one point or another, has been blessed by the same time-less gifts: the chance to lose sleep for months with no idea how to make the noise stop; the chance to hold a newborn; the chance to hear a child say, "Look at me!"

What is the insight from all this? I think the amazing thing about being a parent is that almost every experience is so filled with meaning and emotion. Being a father means standing in the center of life's most extraordinary moments even though they are frequently hidden in the ordinary. In the last twenty-four hours alone, I have seen my daughter Kathleen ride her bike for the first time, to an explosion of joy; I have read a poem written by my daughter Rose for her grandparents that reduced me to tears; I have heard my son Tim exclaim after lashing a line drive, "Hey Dad, I've got my swing back! Yeah, baby!"; I have accepted a beautiful drawing from my son Sam of him and his dad holding hands, ready to play ball; and I have felt my daughter Caroline's two-year-old fingers tighten around my finger as I put her to sleep, wanting me to stay, not letting me go.

I think it all comes down to the simple realization that love is not blind at all but, as Martha Beck has written, probably the only force that allows us to see clearly.

I was taught this lesson recently by a father I admire, though I do not know his name. I met him in Arusha, Tanzania, where I had gone for a Special Olympics event. His son Ramadan, a Special Olympics athlete, met me at the near-deserted airport in the middle of the night and welcomed me with flowers. Ramadan is twenty, has a moderate form of mental retardation, and has health complications that result from malnutrition. On the way to the hotel, the rickety bus stopped along the dark roadside to let Ramadan out, and he disappeared into a field headed toward home.

Days later, the culminating event for our games in Arusha was ready to start, the 10K run. The stadium we were using was filling with spectators because the streets of Arusha are cluttered with the unemployed and those with no where to go. At the start of the race, I saw Ramadan at the line, but then saw his coach telling him, "No, Ramadan. This race is too long for you."

But Ramadan insisted on running through the jagged streets with no sneakers on his feet. I heard his coach relent. The coach then went to Ramadan's father, a dimunitive, expressionless man dressed in a second-hand sport coat that drooped over his shoulders. The coach told him that Ramadan would be allowed to start the race and be picked up by a car when he faltered. His father nodded.

The race was off, and Special Olympics runners from eight countries ran out of the stadium and through the town. For more than thirty minutes, the stadium had no activity, and then the lead runner, Joseph Mateuzu from Zimbabwe, came into the stadium, rounded the track, and finished in a time of thirty-four minutes. Over the next few minutes, one by one, the runners returned as we moved toward the time limit of one hour.

Most of the runners had finished within fifty-five minutes and a lull returned to the crowd. Then, at fifty-nine minutes, the final runner still on the street charged into the stadium. It was Ramadan, and he rounded the outer half of the track and turned down the homestretch as the crowd began to cheer. And down the final hundred meters, with the crowd roaring, he ran, his head high, his chest out; and with all the energy God gave him, he finished. Ramadan finished the race. His coach ran over to me, held my shoulders, and said, "Tim, I am so proud. I am so proud." And I looked over to the side of the track to see Ramadan's father, still expressionless, but with tears streaming down his face, looking at his son with pride.

That father taught *me* that day. He was proud of his son, to be sure. But he was overwhelmed less by what his son did and more by who his son was, less by his skill and more by his attempt, less by his finishing time and more by the spirit he shared. He wept with joy for this boy who had nothing: no education, no real dwelling place, no chance for a job, no real breaks in life. But this boy finished a race that no one thought he could. He made his father proud. He was a gift.

Maybe that, then, is my experience of fatherhood—the experience of God giving me the chance to know that I am being given more than enough, that it is being freely given, that I have done nothing to deserve the joyful flooding of my heart that comes from those children, and maybe most importantly, that I need do nothing to deserve it. It is to know that the ability to be a father comes from the awareness that the Father loves us so completely as to give us children. It is to remember in the words of that most passionate father of Jesus' love parable, the prodigal son: "My son, everything I have is yours."

I invite the fathers and the sons and daughters of fathers to remember your own love stories and return to their simplest message: love completely, without guile, without reserve, just like a father holding a newborn baby. Just like God.

*Tim Shriver is President of Special Olympics. He and his wife Linda Potter have five children: Rose, Tim, Sam, Kathleen, and Caroline.*

# Faith of Our Children

*Franklin J. Havlicek*

For a year I thought about whether to accept this invitation to speak. This was not so much a delaying tactic as a response due to a sense of awe in addressing something more personal, more hidden within me, than I thought I could ever discuss in a public setting.

By this I mean that my father's faith in God in large part led me to become a father, and my children's faith in me as their father led me to rediscover my own faith in a time of difficulty—how inseparably fatherhood and faith are connected in my heart, in my soul.

As a small boy in New York City's borough of Queens, I heard the same question posed over and over again by my mother's many relatives, all of them Italian immigrants: "What do you want to be when you grow up?" I never could find an answer until one day, when I was about five, I said, "When I grow up I want to be a father."

From the reaction of my parents and relatives— "Bravo!"—I knew immediately that it was the right answer. But it took me many more years, until I was forty years old, to achieve my boyhood goal.

My own father, Raymond, gave me every reason to want to be like him. His lifelong, unfailing faith in God, and his self-sacrifice for his children, were the bedrock of my own faith. He was also an "American dream come true" for my mother, Rosalia, and for my sister, my three brothers, and me. He was something of a cowboy, born and raised in Montana, who hitchhiked to Notre Dame for college, served as an infantry captain in the Pacific, and then, while on leave, at the Rockefeller Center skating rink in Manhattan, met my mother, a garment worker from Hell's Kitchen turned New York fashion model.

As you might imagine, my father and mother were very different. My mother sang Italian operas while she cooked and cleaned. And sometimes when he came home from work, my father played the guitar, whistled, and sang cowboy songs. He could even yodel. Ray and Rosie gave all they could of themselves to their five children, saw all five through college, and lived to see them all married. But their differences led to discord and, after years of growing estrangement, to divorce.

My father taught us that love conquers all differences and difficulties, though in fact my parents' differences, at first a source of wonder and pride, led us later to lose faith in the power of love. Often working two jobs, my father alone remained unshaken, always forgiving, offering his love without qualification; his own faith seemed only stirred, not shaken. He showed by his example, less by telling us than by simply bearing his daily burdens, often with a wink and a smile, sometimes a silent prayer, the way to a life of faith.

Just three days after the marriage of his last single child, he died an early and unexpected death at sixty-six that left his children stunned. To our astonishment, comfort came from our father two days later, when a letter he wrote to our sister arrived, saying how much he loved us all.

Thirty-five years after my father's fateful visit to Rockefeller Center, I first spotted Louise Sferrazza, an Italian girl from Queens, on the subway platform at Rockefeller Center, just below the skating rink. We both got off the train at the same stop, West 72nd Street, and found that we had lived on the same block for three years without meeting. It was the evening of December 21, the darkest day of the year. But by the time we had walked to West 75th Street and spoken for a few minutes, it dawned on each of us that we would some day marry.

Three years later, on December 21, we did just that. But it took seven more years, lots of doctors followed by fertility drugs then plans to adopt, before Louise's unlikely pregnancy. Our first child, Lee, is a warm, witty, calm, and graceful girl, with great strength of character and her mother's stubborn good sense. Within moments of her birth, when she pushed the little newborn's cotton cap off her head, it was clear that our brown-eyed, brown-haired girl would be "a feisty one," as the delivery nurse predicted.

Four years after Lee's birth, after a miscarriage and more doctors and drugs, a second miraculous birth took place. It was as unexpected and unique as Lee's. Shortly before Christmas, Louise and I adopted a six-day-old boy, our son, Raymond. He was handed to us with his blue eyes wide open, staring at us with the same amazement we felt. A social worker told us how "wonderful" he was. For us, the Christmas prophecy was fulfilled and given breathtaking new meaning: "Unto us a child is born, a son is given," and he was called "wonderful." Ray is now a lively, thoughtful, somewhat mischievous, redheaded, and big-hearted boy, with a firm sense of himself and his father's sense of humor.

Louise and I love both of our children "more than all the stars in the sky," as Lee used to say as a little girl—or, in Ray's words, "more than googleplex times infinity." The family Louise and I have built together has taken twenty years of marriage—and we didn't marry young! In all that time we also overcame many other obstacles. These have included both of us going to university while working, buying a burned-out Queens row house two days before we married, and moving eight years later to Washington, where we lived through another, three-year reconstruction of our house on Western Avenue. But our troubles were few compared to many others, as life reminds us from time to time.

Several years ago, a severe test of my principles became a kind of crucible for my faith and family. There were real threats to answer, twenty-four-hour security guards at our house, and tough choices to be made. I found myself having to set a new course, both professionally and personally, and wanting to renew our marriage and our family's sense of direction. For the first time in twenty-five years, I stopped working. I wanted it to be the best of times, but it soon seemed dispiriting and filled with worry.

This didn't feel like a "career transition," as it is often called, but an accumulation of all the losses I had ever sustained—as a boy, losing my only pair of gloves in winter, and having to collect old newspapers in the neighborhood to help buy new ones; as a student, losing my heroes to assassination, including Robert Kennedy, for whom I worked; as a soldier during Vietnam who served in Germany, losing my illusions about glory, but not my life; or as a young lawyer losing my first trial representing my father and, too soon after, losing my father himself.

I began to wonder about my full-speed, hard-working, come-what-may way of life. As the weeks went by, I lost my bearings. There were no stars in the sky. Nothing before had left me feeling so hopeless, though I prayed every day for help, without faith in anything. I thought about my father's hard times, losing his twenty-seven-year job then his thirty-two-year marriage in quick succession, after which he moved to a house in the Adirondack wilderness area in upstate New York for several years. I thought about my father's father, who lost three sons between the ages of six and twelve within a year, but who then moved from Minnesota to Montana, where they had three more sons, the seventh and last my father.

Maybe, I thought, I should move my father some place new. I found myself talking late into the night, sometimes all night, with Louise, a few friends and family, particularly my remarkable sister, Sarah, and my other father, my father-in-law, Charlie, who came to stay with us for a time. With our children, Louise and I drove cross-country—where else?—to Montana, where we visited relatives and saw my father's old friends, breathed mountain air and saw the sky full of stars at night, before returning to Washington. But financial fears and other worries still weighed heavily, and my job search felt like Job's helpless search.

After months of deepening uncertainty, something happened, something almost inexpressible, that I know was decisive. Though there were times when I know our children found my worries frightening, most of all because I was worried and home all the time, and not "at work," I saw that they never, ever lost their faith in me. Their love never wavered—never could, because I was their father. Sometimes, when I found myself walking around the house very late, Lee would wake up just to give me a kiss, then fall back to sleep. Ray would tell me almost every day how glad he was that I was at home for the first time, to take him to school and play with him afterward, and that he wanted me to stay home "forever."

I recalled how Louise's and my faith in God made it possible to keep trying for years to have each of our children. And I prayed harder than ever, not for myself, but as Lee and Ray's father.

There was no sign of God's grace other than what had been there all along—in my children's faith in me. Their love came to us as parents through our love for one another. It is part of one love all of us share with God, but it is different, closer to God's love for us than ours for them. How grateful Louise and I are to the Father of us all for the love of Lee and Ray.

*Franklin J. Havlicek works at an international organization and is an adjunct professor of International and Public Affairs at American University in Washington, D.C. He and his wife Louise have two children, Lee Karel and Raymond.*

# The Little Girl Who Came to Stay

*John Lenczowski*

The most striking events of my life as a father were the actual births of my children, Katie and Christian. Despite my general faith in God, I had never fully appreciated the degree to which our lives are in his hands. But their births made me understand that each human being is a miraculous creation of the Lord and is therefore worthy of all the respect that the commandment "Love your neighbor" requires of us.

Until you have your first child, you don't fully appreciate the extent of the responsibility. When our daughter was born, we quickly realized that she was the little girl who came to stay. We would wake up in the middle of the night and realize that she was still there.

When I became a father, I was touched by so many of the gifts that my children brought to my life—their innocence and their trust, the joy of watching them learn new things about the world, and the constant surprise of their ideas, their art work, their imaginary play, and their sense of humor. I was also amazed to see how they were born with unique personalities and how these personalities were innate and not determined by their environment.

When your child is born, it puts everything else in perspective. It compels you to readjust your priorities. It shatters your propensity to remain self-absorbed. It makes you call upon your best instincts of unselfishness. It inspires you to provide your children with a good example. What once seemed to be the most important thing professionally suddenly can become secondary. By making you care about your children's future, fatherhood makes you more concerned about the general well-being and moral fabric of the society that will surround them.

Fatherhood has also impressed upon me how accurate the concept of original sin is. From their youngest years, children demonstrate that human beings have the capacity to do other than good. And this taught me what a continuous effort it is to guide our children down the right path.

Given the fallen nature of man, we see how constant is the battle to preserve civilization. It takes only one generation of neglect to witness a significant deterioration of social behavior.

As my children have grown, I have realized that I have only one chance to do my job well as a father. Since this has turned out to be the Lord's plan for me, he has entrusted me with sharing in the most important task of my children's upbringing: to help shape their character and conscience, and to give them the tools by which they can undertake their greatest responsibilities, namely, to know and love the Lord and to follow his rules of life.

The most important part of this task is to show my children what it means to give unconditional love. This involves nothing less than giving them a taste of how unconditional God's love is for them.

A large part of this—and perhaps one of the most important elements of fatherhood—is to let my children see my own love for my wife, Susan, and to see how I support her in her own job as their mother. This involves, among other things, expressing appreciation for her tireless efforts and conveying it to our children. Parents showing respect for one another is the first step in teaching children respect.

While mothers have their own daunting challenges, so do fathers—if they are to do their job well. Since so much of fatherhood involves helping to shape moral character, much of this must be done by serving as a role model. But modern life is such that fathers have been less able to serve this function than in the past. And I am not just talking about the culture of fatherlessness that has plagued parts of our city and country.

As James Stenson has written, in contrast to earlier periods, children today rarely see their fathers working and being given respect by other adults. They don't regularly see those virtues that manifest themselves in professional life: displaying courage, overcoming obstacles and disappointments, competing honorably, and setting and achieving goals and the like.*

Meanwhile, too many children develop their concepts of adulthood from television, and television's puerile adults

---

*James B. Stenson, *Successful Fathers* (Princeton, NJ: Scepter Publishers, 1994).

serve as role-model competition for real fathers. Add to this the increasing toxicity of television shows and the power of peer pressure, and the number of influences competing with fathers is prodigious indeed.

Clearly we fathers need all the help we can get. And the real source of that help, I believe, has to come from the Lord's inspiration.

He has given us several opportunities to harness his help. One is through the image of God that we convey to our children. Our own attitude toward God is the one that we can shape in our children's minds. And we can do this by leading our families in the sacramental life and by sharing prayer with our children.

We can also set a good example in the way we treat them and others; in the way we exhibit patience, self-control, forgiveness, and other virtues; in the way we respect them, show our interest in them, and listen to their ideas; in the way we spend our time, express our opinions, and teach them to behave properly while showing mercy and understanding. All of these are expressions of love that cannot be given unless one makes time, even when there is no time.

Having been blessed to grow up in relatively privileged circumstances, I have seen how prosperity has made many of us too comfortable in thinking that we have created all this material well-being by ourselves. When you are comfortable, you rarely call upon the Lord for help.

Having been personally involved in a risky entrepreneurial venture—setting up a new school—I have had to call upon his help more often than most. And I have been struck again and again by what I can only rationally explain as his intervention in sustaining my work. So my children have been able to see a glimpse of their father's faith. I believe that this can only be of help in the process of their own moral formation.

*John Lenczowski, former adviser on Soviet affairs for President Reagan, is founder and director of The Institute of World Politics in Washington, D.C. He and his wife Susan have two children, Katie and Christian.*

# Don't Tell Anybody How Much You Love Me!

## *Jose M. Herrero*

When I told my wife about speaking as a father, she became very concerned. I am not a native English speaker. I am too emotional, too passionate. Right away, she gave me the following advice: "Please do not tell everybody how much you love me, tell everybody that you have no regrets about being a father, and be brief. No more than five minutes, please!"

Please look at your watches now. If I am still speaking five minutes from now, very discreetly you can start coughing or raising your arm and pointing at your watch. I will not be offended.

My children told me to tell you how proud I am of them. True. And even more importantly, I have to tell everybody in this parish that I am absolutely crazy about my children.

For almost a month I have been asking other fathers for advice on what to say. One of the best suggestions I got came from one of my friends in Washington who has two adopted children. He told me to listen to God and ask him, "What should I tell you today?" And I ask God in this very moment to please help me and my English.

In the Bible, we have some interesting things to learn about fathers. For example, God as our father worked six days and six nights to create the universe and our planet Earth with its oceans, continents, rivers, and mountains. He created us humans and loves us so much that he gave us his Son, Jesus Christ, as our most dependable friend.

*Lesson:* Fathers are people who enjoy creating things.

Adam was kind of a hippie hanging out in Paradise with his wife, not much to do, and he just messed things up when he ate that apple.

*Lesson:* Fathers sometimes make terrible mistakes, and for that matter, so do children! Let's be patient and compassionate about our children's mistakes.

Abraham got carried away a little bit thinking that God wanted him to kill his son.

*Lesson:* Fathers sometimes misinterpret what God wants them to do with their children.

Saint Joseph is one of my favorite fathers in the Bible. He was a nice guy. He raised Jesus Christ even though he was not his real son.

*Lesson:* Fathers should treat other children as their own.

The last father I remember was the one described in the parable of the lost son. A young man asked his father for half of all his assets; he gave it to him, then the son runs away and spends it all. And when he was broke, he came back home and his father was overjoyed.

*Lesson:* Fathers must be forgiving and must love their children no matter what they do.

My own father had twelve children. I am number eleven; for almost five years, I was the baby in the family until my sister came and took my place.

My father was a good and kind man, an outstanding scholar, a Spanish-Civil-War veteran, a governor for fifteen years. He said the rosary every single day of his life with my mother and raised our family with no television. Sixteen priests co-celebrated Mass at his funeral.

The most incredible time with my father was the ten minutes I spent with him at home just before he died, holding his hand. The two of us were alone in his bedroom while the rest of the family was having dinner. My father gave me the honor to escort him in the very last lap of his journey to heaven. Although this may sound strange to some of you, the two most memorable and joyful moments of my life have been seeing my children's coming into this world and witnessing my father's departure from it.

Dad, this is your son—happy Father's Day. I love you more than I have ever loved you before. I think of you often. I am very proud to have you as my father. Sorry for all the times I disappointed you.

My mother and father raised us in Madrid, Spain. But the role of fathers in this society is different. I enjoy and accept the challenges that fatherhood brings to my life here. I agree with Bill Cosby in his book *Fatherhood* that the only thing we men cannot do is get pregnant, deliver children, and breast feed. Outside of that, everything else in raising a family can be done and should be done with husband and wife as a team. There is not one, but many different ways of being a father. Nobody has the last say on fatherhood. Every single day I look forward to coming home and giving a hug to my children, Clara and Gaby, because I love them very, very much.

I was at the 1992 Olympics, which were celebrated in Barcelona, Spain. The most beautiful moment of the opening ceremonies was the archer shooting a flaming arrow, aiming it toward the Olympic torch to be lit. Kahlil Gibran in *The Prophet* sees God as the archer, us fathers as the bow, and the children as arrows: "Let your bending in the archer's hand be for gladness."

*Jose M. Herrero is a lawyer and U.S. program director for Comillas University of Madrid, Spain. He and his wife Jane Raybould have two children, Clara and Gaby.*

# Doing This "Life Thing"

## *Michael E. Zielinski*

My first encounter with the thought of my own father-hood occurred one afternoon in the fall of 1975. Judy and I had been married for two years and had bought our first and present home the year before. She wasn't feeling partic-ularly perky and had gone in for a check up. She called me at work and said, "I guess we'll have to buy a station wagon." The message immediately clicked. I knew that her gynecologist had just given her a room full of furniture. Then she just said it: "I'm pregnant." I don't remember what I said.

There was a note of happy excitement in her voice, and I was excited, too. I thought, maybe, at the age of thirty-one, I'm actually growing up and will become a real adult.

I didn't stop to think (it was too late by then anyway) about disruptions to income stream and free time and why I wouldn't have a car to drive to work. I think God pro-grammed us that way; we sometimes call it nature. One thing just leads to another and...there you are.

As the magic day approached—June 17, 1976—we grew increasingly excited. We bought an 8mm movie-sound camera (this was before video camcorders were affordable). We burned at least twelve rolls of film on pre-birth stuff—mostly imperceptible steps on the road to delivery, like a small protrusion on stretched abdominal skin.

Relax. I didn't bring the film with me. It is probably the mother of boring home movies. We actually showed the whole thing to some friends of ours who did not protest or walk out. That was a true definition of friendship. For a couple of years, we were so devoted and focused that we actually enjoyed watching it. We probably will a few years from now, too.

After Kristin's birth, Allison came two years later, though two months early. She weighed in at three pounds, went down to two-and-a-half, and spent the first two months of her life in Georgetown Hospital's "preemie" unit. That quickly brought us to the realization that this procreation thing wasn't the slam dunk that we thought it was.

Fortunately Alli, who had a miraculous recovery from a heart problem just when things were getting a little dicey, turned out fine, and we went on our way trying to figure out how to raise children.

It's peculiar: I don't recall that being a real stressful time in my life, though it was. I am an incurable optimist. I don't know whether that is a protective mechanism to avoid stress, or whether it is a recognition that Judy can easily stress out enough for both of us. Whatever the reason, many of these things have been much easier on me than they have on her, and I have some guilt about that. But I digress.

Fleeing her emotionally stressful job as a superior-court social worker, Judy quit working outside the home, and we became the old classic "SIDK," or Single-Income, Double Kids.

Now I have to admit—having four sisters and no brothers—I'm probably brainwashed, but mothers have it much harder than fathers. My day-to-day life changed, of course, but not nearly as much as Judy's. I continued to go to work; she stayed home. Most of the real "parenting" duties fell squarely on her shoulders: monitoring health, nursing through sickness, disciplining, most of the things that young children will imprint from their adult role models. That is a lot of responsibility.

As they progressed into and through Blessed Sacrament School, I coached softball and basketball for some of their Catholic Youth Organization (CYO) teams and watched them flower into kids who loved that game and would nail down that full-ride scholarship to the university of their choice. Well, almost—but with me as a coach, what could you expect?

When I was trying to put my thoughts together on what fatherhood meant to me, I looked up the word *father* in the dictionary. It wasn't very helpful. The first and obvious definition was "male parent." The qualifications to attain fatherhood, in themselves, are not too demanding under that definition.

Looking further, most of the other definitions were essentially the equivalent of simple fatherhood—*originator, inventor, creator.* The only word that seemed close to my idea of fatherhood, or what this day is about, was *protector.*

Notably absent were concepts like *nurture.* You guessed it—that comes under motherhood. But *nurture* should be in the definition. So should *counsel* and *guide.* That they aren't is probably attributable to the fact that men wrote these things and wanted to keep the real tough stuff in the motherhood area. *Provide*—which seems to be sliding into the motherhood area these days—should be there, too.

I tried to do a little self-evaluation of how I have done so far as a father. It's a mixed bag. Since things seem to have gone pretty well, there is a temptation to say, "Good job," and leave it at that. I hesitate to do that though, because most of this is probably the result of Judy's efforts in the first place, and some of it may be just heredity, beyond my own efforts.

I think I handled the "protector thing" pretty well. The girls have not been carried off by the wild beasts of Chevy Chase, Maryland. On the other hand, there are many dangers out there that you can't protect them from, such as the decline in moral values, the increase in drugs and sexual promiscuity, and so on. The best you can do is provide some immunization through example.

Provider? Not as much as I—or they—would probably like. We have the basics and we'll get them close to half way through college, mainly because of some money that Judy's mother left her. Nurturer? Room for improvement there. I have left much of that job to Judy.

I also have to admit that, as a husband and a parent, God has not presented me with great challenges. In his wisdom, he has accommodated my shortcomings, for which I am thankful. I have been blessed with a loyal, caring, responsible wife, my spiritual anchor. Our children are healthy, excellent students, and well-behaved, at least in the broad sense of the phrase. For example, neither of them has threatened to drop out of school and run off with a skinhead/militia group.

There are new challenges, and will continue to be. We are still learning to deal with the teenage "independence thing," when they seem at times to have a negative reaction to anything you are interested in, and don't want to be seen with you in public. That seems to be resolving itself some now. The realization that they are on the verge of adulthood themselves—truly independent from us—is a little disquieting.

So there you have it: one pretty unremarkable story of fatherhood.

What it boils down to, in my mind, is a long-term project. You start out knowing nothing at all about what you are doing. You play it by ear, and you take it one step at a time. If you're lucky, God makes sure that there is a rock where your feet come down to keep you from drowning.

I believe that in raising children you can't control the outcome; you can just hope to influence it in a positive way. The most important thing is to try and live a good example. We have been involved members of a faith community and will continue to be. There should be a nugget of faith in our children that will be of great value to them as they move into their adulthood and, hopefully, face the same challenges that we did.

I also believe that parenting—fatherhood and motherhood—is probably the most important thing that people who are fortunate enough to have children can do. It is the best thing that has happened to me. I can't conceive of doing this "life thing" any other way.

*Michael E. Zielinski is a U.S. administrative law judge who hears mine safety and healthcases. He and his wife Judith have two daughters, Kristin, a graduate of the University of Virginia, and Allison, a graduate of Georgetown University.*

# A Better Man

*Gregory Orfalea*

### Covering a Child

Early, before the sun wins me
I check how you all look sleeping.
One is always wrapped
too tightly, and one on the floor
because he does not like to sleep
alone in the room
we prepared for him
but with his brothers. And one
is exposed to the last hunger
of the night. It is this one
I cover with a sheet only,
though the first draft of fall
breathes through the screen.
And I wonder: Will he always be
exposed? What winter will find him
with too thin a sweater?
What woman with too thin
a heart will try to cover him?
He does not move. I love them,
plunged in their separate dreams
together. The door closes

quietly as the night
removes its cover
from a father.

To be a father is to be connected. It's also, I think, a state of being without cover or giving up cover. It's not a role for the squeamish or anyone interested in hiding or hoarding or, for that matter, making it to the top. A father's work is most often done at ground level.

My last book was a kind of double memoir of my own father and his ill-fated unit in the Second World War. I have a photo of him as the motorcycle messenger of his battalion. He is wearing an Army cap, not a helmet, while on his motorcycle. And like that wool cap, it is the sense of protection and exposure that to me is the essence of being a father. We are exposed as parents, but also exalted in that exposure.

Obviously I am a word-tinkerer. I fiddle with words and some people even pay me to fiddle. But that doesn't matter. What matters, and is really the best thing I can say for myself, is that in 1984, Eileen Rogers took a chance on me in a little ceremony at Dahlgren Chapel at Georgetown University, and I became, beyond my wildest dreams, the father of three great sons—Matthew, Andrew, and Luke.

There is something daunting about this. Nothing I can do, really, nothing I can whip up in words, or planks of wood, or edifices of money, can ever match this simple, yet profound life I never expected to have. I came to the table late, thirty-four. I always call Eileen my "eleventh-hour rescue." Does this mean I should just shut down the shop and declare victory? Hardly. You earn this miracle of fatherhood and husbandhood the rest of your life. What's truly exciting about being a father is being open to the wonder of our children's lives, to learn from them, to help them learn the road of life, in turn; and in the process, one has a chance to become something one never thought possible: a better man. It's a great bargain. It will only cost you your life—that is, your old, dusty life of self. I recommend it to anyone.

Eileen has cautioned me not to forget those men who could not become fathers. There is, of course, more to being a father than biology—witness the fatherhood of our parish priests. I think especially of my Uncle Jerry Unrein, the German in our family who could cool off our pack of Arabs. Indeed, when I was growing up, Uncle Jerry and Aunt Bette, who did not have children of their own, lived three doors down from us in Anaheim, California, on a little street called Nutwood. Each day, it seems, I visited them and received things like hot cocoa or cold water, and always, always, kindness and wisdom. I feel I was raised by two sets of parents. Uncle Jerry was a labor negotiator, and I learned much from his ability to be a go-between and to seek compromise between warring parties. He also had a great sense of sometimes gently risque humor, telling my sneezing dad, "Aref, that's a helluva honker!" and calling me "Tiger."

Humor in uncomfortable situations. Or facing a predicament in which there is no good choice, no easy out, in fact, *no* out. This leads me to contemplate my own father and his army unit in the Second World War.

The 551st Parachute Infantry Battalion, for whose commander my father was the messenger, sustained one of the worst casualty rates—84 percent—of any such unit at the Battle of the Bulge. Over the eight years I worked on the book about the unit and Dad, I had the privilege of meeting the survivors, many of whom reminded me of my father with their wry self-effacement, generosity, and succinct wisdom. Both my father and his lost battalion—whose records were misplaced and whose achievement was long forgotten— faced a terrible brink in the war, and my father one in peace- time. But it is there at the brink that you find out who you really are.

People sometimes ask me why I wear such a heavy, double-sized wedding band. Well, it's not one band; it's two. After my father was killed in 1985, someone put it in my hand and I instinctively slipped it on alongside my own. Eileen and I had been married only a year. The two are together; I don't take them off. And I don't quite know how to explain my father's death except to say he was done in by friendly fire, and I figured he needed a friend. An unflinching one. Or I did.

It's hard to talk about my father even now after I've written a book about his life in the war and, in a sense, his greatest battle in peacetime with a child's mental illness, an illness which ultimately took her life and his. It's not hard to reel off my father's physical courage—the parachuting, the motorcycling, the deep-sea spear fishing—but it is his spiri- tual courage that sticks with me most, that awes me until this day. He just never gave up.

During a long unemployment, after building up and los- ing a million-dollar dress-manufacturing business, he came to visit me in Washington, D.C., when I was living alone in a threadbare apartment. The night after he left, I arrived back at the apartment expecting to be very lonely and saw that he had sewn colorful drapes for each window, like an oyster depositing his pearl. He combated despair by giving.

Few if any of us, pray God, will ever be faced with the irreducible hell my father faced just before he died at sixty. But one thing parenthood means, whether in extreme circumstances or just the normal trials of everyday life, is this: we are here for the duration. It's important for me to let my sons know that, wind, rain, or bad grades, as a father, I am here for them. They can rely on me. I may not approve of some things they do. I may, like *my* father, pop my cork in anger and say things I don't mean. But my love for them is ever-ready. It will not die. It is a blessed constant, a gift to me as much as to them, as natural a wonder as their coming into this world.

I remember my father once bought a one-way ticket to Tahiti. He'd pretty much had it. He was tempted to flee. He might be alive today if he had. But he wouldn't have been Aref Orfalea. The ticket was returned.

Can I live up to the example of his extraordinary selflessness? I'm not sure. When the job is poor or downsized, or the temper short, or the writing impossible, or the house closing in, a slow boat to China looks awfully enticing. But I know I am best a father when I persevere, when I can be leaned on, even when my insides are churning.

My father's faith was important to him. He was anything but sanctimonious, however, and preferred the back of the church. In fact, I think he was of the "last shall be first, first shall be last" variety of man. My mother would often beeline to the front pews, and my father would whisper, "Rose? Where in God's name are you going?" "To hear God's name," she would reply. My father, no doubt, heard God's name best in the back.

Again, his faith was not without faltering. As my sister's illness got worse, he would leave Mass early and smoke outside. And yet I cannot forget how, with his own hands, he forged a backyard grotto to the Blessed Mother out of brick; how we used to kneel together to say the rosary during Lent in front of a crucifix in the living room; how he loved St. Joseph, his patron saint as his middle name was Joseph. St. Francis de Sales tells us that St. Joseph died out of sheer love from seeing the Creator in his Son's eyes.

What have I taken forward in my own faith from my parents? So little, it seems. And yet I try. For many years, I would sing the boys to sleep with "O Salutaris Hostia" and "Tantum Ergo" as my mother did to me. Never underestimate the lulling rhythms of a dead language! So little of faith can be spoken or ordered. It can only be shown.

My father showed it best in his ability to admit wrong. Once, during the Vietnam War protest years, when I was arguing some sort of arrogant position and spoke curtly to my mother, he jumped up and chased me around the breakfast room. I had to hold him off with a chair like a lion-tamer. I ran out of the house thinking he was cuckoo, and took refuge at my Aunt Jeanette's house. When I returned later that night, I got in bed and tried to fall asleep. The door opened to my bedroom and in came my father, who sat on the corner of my bed and whispered, "Gregory, if I ever do anything like that again, you leave with mom and the other kids. Because I don't deserve you." I leapt up in bed and hugged him hard. I pray for that kind of honesty and courage.

Though we were often taken for brothers when I was growing up, in some ways I am a different kind of person and father than my father was, certainly facing a different set of familial problems. I am more bookish than my dad and am not nearly as good with my hands as he was. He could sink his own sprinkler system in the yard, build a fence, run a tractor and motorcycle, cut a stack of cloth with a cutter's blade. A Midwesterner at heart (born and raised in Cleveland), he was all contact in his sports—football and ice hockey; I stuck with basketball, baseball, and tennis. I recall his being too busy to come to most of my high school games (mother filled the breach), whereas, like most of my generation of fathers, I have dived knee-deep in my children's athletics. It makes me ponder whether or not we are all trying too hard to recapture our youth, something my father's generation never seemed to even consider.

Dad never went to college; he married a Syrian girl from his own community in Los Angeles; he lived with a large extended family support system tapped every Sunday. I married an Irish girl three thousand miles from home partly because I was flung that far to college. The only thing that took my father away from his roots was war. And when it was over, when he moved—from Cleveland to Los Angeles—virtually the entire tribe moved with him. Being far away from the warmth of a large extended family in California raising my own little family has not been easy, but it has had its virtues. It instilled a paradoxical independence and closeness in us, a savoring of our own new brood as we depended more on each other, perhaps, than would have been the case in the throng. I steeped myself in a different life with different rhythms—that of my good in-laws and wife. Being far from the love I had known as a boy called out new things in me, provided new joys and places of endearment. "Matthew Hill" is near the Washington Zoo; "Andrew Point" is down by the Tidal Basin and the Jefferson Memorial; "Luke Tunnel" is in Rock Creek Park.

Though, early in our marriage, we were literally shocked into place in the East by the violent loss of my father and sister out West, over time a loneliness crept into me, a sorrow at being so far away as to be of little use to anyone back home. Raising children and all its demands and joys cut that loneliness, to be sure, transformed it even, but as you age, and they age and are poised to leave, the pull of original life and ties is strong. On the other hand, touch wood, I have not had to deal—as my father did—with the free fall of a child to mental illness, violence, and suicide. Our Luke has neurofibromatosis, which causes him significant learning disabilities, but that is a far gentler problem than what my father faced.

I have emphasized here the harder realities of being a father, the imponderables presented to a father. But truly the boys have been a source of great wonder and inspiration to me. They, too, have shown courage. I'll never forget when, on hearing that his second-grade teacher had been killed in a car crash, our son Andy, who had only just begun to learn to ride a bike, hopped on it and, fighting off the tears, yelled, "This is for Ms. Hill!" He circled Lafayette Elementary School's track eight times without stopping. He'd only gone around once before. Or Luke's first relay race in the Special Olympics, or his great victory of speaking after not speaking for the first four years of his life. Luke's gift of loving, his patented "Sure!" to almost any plan for food or travel shimmers throughout our days. I cannot imagine him being "normal." I would not want him any other way. As for Matthew, his tenacity, his refusal to be discouraged after a dip in grades, and his hard work to bring them up have been a wonder. The day he cut me a piece of cake after an argument. His rescuing suggestions of "Let's take a walk, Dad."

There are those days when everything is just buoyant, and an unexpected equilibrium is reached—have you had them? Watching the children saunter home on a crisp and clear day, you suddenly venture to yourself, certainly not spoken, barely breathed, "This is happiness. How did this happen to me? I am lucky to be alive." It passes, of course, as it must pass. But that does not deny its force. I have felt it at times at Mass, as the children move with their cans of food at the Offertory, amid the murmurs and coughs, a great feeling that I belong. For all I have lost, this I gained.

I will end with a poem of worship. It's for Eileen, without whom fatherhood and so many other joys would be impossible.

## Sunday Morning

Entering you, half-awake,
half-enveloped by the past,
loving you, half astride,
half-aware what will live will not last.

Holding you, chalice up,
before the children's first cry
in February, halfway to spring,
this would be a good way to die.

But living, and knowing there is more life
to live, more bones to crack,
more heartache to mend and bring back,
I give great thanks for what I lack.

My lack brought me you, and what you see:
the cardinal in the winter tree!

*Gregory Orfalea has written six books and teaches writing at Pitzer College in Claremont, California. He and his wife Eileen, a realtor, have three sons: Matthew, Andrew, and Luke.*

# Get Back Up on That Truck

*Andrew Greene*

I think of one personal story every time the subject of fatherhood comes up. I was a relatively new father, living in Baltimore with my wife and son. I was a route supervisor for Pepsi-Cola in a tough part of the city, earning a very modest wage. We lived a simple, sometimes hard life.

Suddenly I became confused about what the future had in store for us. I lost a great deal of hope for a better life, the kind of life that my wife and I had dreamed of. It is so painful to lose hope.

I felt I desperately needed a change. One day, covering one of my salesmen's routes, I finally had had enough. I pulled over on a city block, climbed down, picked up a pay phone, and called my dad collect. As always, he stopped what he was doing and picked up when he knew it was me.

I slowly began explaining that things were becoming very discouraging for me. I felt that I was not moving ahead anymore and that the road was not getting any easier. I felt that I was letting my beautiful young family down. Things simply were not adding up as I thought they would. I fell into a desperate inner struggle. Finally I just broke down and cried.

My dad listened patiently to my blubbering, and when I gave him the opportunity to speak, he said a few words that I still repeat to myself everyday. He took a deep breath, one that I've heard so often, and said, "I understand. Now you get back up on that truck and finish what you started. Give it everything you have, and when we get together again soon, we can spend a few minutes re-evaluating the situation. You keep moving, Andrew. Do you hear me? Keep moving forward."

I was scared that day. Thinking back, I could not imagine how tough it was for Dad to hang up that phone and continue his day productively. I am sure that he found a way.

I once shared this story with a relative, who coolly observed, "Well, that's your dad's tough love." I disagree. There was nothing tough about his love that day. After some time to reflect on the conversation, I found myself filling up with enthusiasm, pride, encouragement, and hope. In the weeks that followed, my confidence grew stronger and stronger. It was the love that Dad had given *before* that day on the phone that made me feel so wonderful. It was the hugs, the kisses, and the times Dad told me he loved me *before* that day, that made his message so clear and appropriate. That is what ran through my head when I climbed back in that truck.

Over the years, my father has gone to great lengths and sacrifice to show me how much he loves me. More important than any sacrifice was the fact that he listened to me and spent time with me. He let me watch him and was not afraid to tell me the things he was good at as well as the things he was not so good at. He had taken time to know me, to know me so well, that at the exact moment when I needed him and just the right message, with no time to prepare, he had the words that fit me perfectly.

In just a sentence, he plucked me from a deep pit and put me on safe ground. I say those words when I wake up every day: "Get back up on that truck. Keep moving forward." It may have been advice that many fathers might give their sons, but it was advice that was for me from him. It was mine.

I knew that I could trust him, not because he is smart or had done great things professionally, but because he had spent time with me. He knew me. He was my fan. He came to my soccer games. He came to my swim meets. He has rooted for me all my life. I'm pleased to say I've come a long way since I got out of the truck that day.

As my children grow older, I can begin to identify some of the real wisdom of fatherhood. As a new father, I searched and searched for the "right" way to do everything and the "right" answers. I searched and still search for the right solutions, to the point that I sometimes fail to look at the beautiful answers right at my side: my children. They rarely need any formulas from me, just my time, my concern, and my unconditional love.

Sometimes I fail to see that my children are unique, that they are not me and not my wonderful wife. They are their own selves and need answers and advice unique to them. It is easy to know this, but like so many things, it is not always easy to act on it. They need time, time without an agenda or objective.

I think that, for me, my failure to spend "good" time (time not worrying about work and life) with my children began as soon, I became a father. I was so scared and clumsy. I hate how afraid I was.

Don't be afraid. Support a new, clumsy dad every chance you get. A smile or pat on the back in church or in a store goes a long way to a young man trying to find his way in the world, thinking that he needs to find the way for his entire family as well. When you support new dads, it helps a whole generation of people! A confident father can do so many great things!

I hope that I will be a better father: a father who listens enough, a father who knows enough about his kids that he can really help them and contribute to their lives when they need him, a father who doesn't have to "take time" for his kids, but one who knows: *they are my time.*

***Andrew Greene*** *is a financial consultant. He and his wife Mary Beth have four children: Morley, Mary Jane, Kathleen, and Peter.*

# Don't Overbook Them

## *Mark Hallam*

Oscar Wilde once said, "Fathers should be neither seen nor heard. That is the only proper basis for family life." I guess my family life is not proper, because I feel my role as father is the most important job that I will have. If you ever look through the obituary section in the paper, you always find the deceased referred to as "beloved father," "beloved mother," "beloved husband," or "beloved wife." They never say "beloved investment banker" or "beloved Internet mogul." While a father's role as bread-winner is obviously crucial, and a successful career helps to set the right example for his children, it is important to keep our priorities straight.

My own father served as an excellent role model for me. Raised during the Depression, my father survived polio as a child and went on to serve in the Navy during World War II. I have tried to set a similar strong example for my children, but it gets a little complicated these days as the rise of two-income families has changed to a large degree the traditional roles of father and mother. Responsibilities in many cases overlap.

Well, how does one become a good father? The answer is different for each person. But the first step is to make time for your children. While doing activities together as a family, make a point of doing things alone with each child. This way you can have a one-on-one conversation and get to know each one better. Shakespeare said in *The Merchant of Venice,* "It is a wise father who knows his own child." While keeping the parent-child hierarchy intact, it is still vital to get to know your child more personally, to find out what is going on in his or her life.

If you don't have open communication with your children, it is impossible to find out when they are having problems, and what you can do to help them. Along the same lines, you want your children to feel comfortable enough to come to you with a problem. So returning videos or going to the grocery store, take one of your kids along and attempt to catch up with him or find out what is happening in her life. If one of your kids has made a mistake, the mere act of explaining a problem to you will make the child feel better, and you can then decide what action should be taken.

If you have enough time to go to Starbuck's every day, or to go jogging or golfing, or to surf the Internet, then you should also have time for your children. It doesn't take a village; it just takes a little bit of individual attention to make a world of difference in a child's life.

On the subject of time, while it is always a good idea to keep children active, try not to schedule so many activities that your child gets stressed out and doesn't have time to be a kid or to do his or her homework. Maybe restricting or refocusing your child's outside activities might improve his or her schoolwork or attitude. Few kids are going to get college athletic scholarships; maybe one child in a whole community will ever earn a living in sports. It might be a good idea to have a child focus on one or two sports that he or she likes and leave time for other things.

It is important to find time to do things with your kids other than drive them nonstop from one game to another. While I can't remember every meet I swam in, or every little league baseball or football game I played in, I can certainly remember every vacation my family took while I was growing up, and every Washington Senators or Redskins game that my father took me to. Once again, it is important to keep your priorities straight and make "quality time" available for your kids.

Now before anyone gets the idea that I think I know it all, I'll be the first one to admit that I don't. I think everybody has to determine for themselves what being a good father or parent is and then take action accordingly. I work late a lot, play golf on weekends, and sometimes take golfing trips away from my family. It is an ongoing effort to make time for my children. At a recent meeting for fathers and sons at Blessed Sacrament, one of the exercises was to answer a series of questions on your own, and then try to guess your son's answers, and vice-versa. I thought I knew my son Andrew well, but on the question of what he wanted to be when he grew up, I said, "Andrew, you want to be a doctor or lawyer, right?" Andrew looked at me and said, "Dad, you know I want to work with you in your business," as if it were the most obvious thing in the world. While feeling somewhat silly for not knowing my son as well as I thought I did, his answer also showed me that I wasn't doing too bad a job as father.

*Mark Hallam, a construction subcontractor, and his wife Margaret have a daughter Caroline, and twin sons Matthew and Andrew.*

# Each Child Teaches

## John Donahue

Our five children teach me every day, each in his or her own way, how to be a father. But it wasn't always assured that I would learn.

My wife and I were married several years before we had children. During that time I developed ideas and expectations of how and what I would do when I became a father. But God wanted to teach me something different.

I had some medical problems, and at one point a doctor told me, "Well, I think we can fix you, but I don't know about your being able to have kids." Those are hard words to hear, so I did then what I had always done, I prayed. I prayed: "Lord, what is this about? Is this what you want for me? I don't get it; help me understand." Somehow I received the hope and trust I desperately needed. And wonder of wonders, we began having children.

With that first child I realized that it may be my flesh and blood, but it's God's child. So I gave thanks and I prayed again, "Lord, help me understand how to develop this child as you want." So he sent me a second child, one with all my behaviors, the positives and the negatives. I realized that the Lord wanted me to understand myself completely in order to teach these children.

So I gave thanks but confessed to God, "I'm sorry. I can do better."

The Lord responded, "You need to learn about being sorry." Thus a third child arrived, and with that child I began to recognize forgiveness, because there was an intensity and focus with this one. I had to learn what it meant to forgive with unconditional love. I believe I grew closer to the Lord, and gave thanks.

But the Lord wasn't done with me, because forgiveness has two elements: forgiving and being forgiven. Thus came child number four, and with child number four came a kindness. I experienced being forgiven my own shortcomings. I've watched others in the family experience the same thing, and I realized that this is what the Lord means by forgive and forget.

By this point, we had four children and I was worn out, completely out of patience. So I prayed, and I asked the Lord to give me patience. And it arrived in the form of brown hair and blue eyes. What was really interesting about number five was how the other kids wanted to help. Even with the smallest task they became helpful. But what was more interesting was discovering that joy and humor chase away impatience.

Those are just a few of the things that I've learned. I've only been at this for about eleven years. I'm not a rookie, but I'm certainly not a veteran either. So I'll continue to grow and learn about being a father. I know that there is no recipe to follow, no one way to do things. I experience the stresses and anxiety that come with the job. I do take comfort and have confidence in the fact that as I evaluate, teach, make the decisions that I hope are right and appropriate, pray, and move forward, Christ has guaranteed he is there with me until the end.

*Civil engineers **John Donahue** and his wife Angela have five children: Pete, Jessica, Mallory, Kelsey, and Caitlin.*

# Setting the Stage for God

*Philip McGovern*

My initial reaction to being asked to share some thoughts on what it means to be a father was, "You're kidding, right?" Let me start by saying that I've been studying and experimenting with this thing called fatherhood for only eight years now. So I don't consider myself an expert on the subject by any means, more a student.

I do consider my role as a father to be my vocation. And I believe that it is God's grace that has brought me to this moment. I know that I have been blessed in a number of ways. I've had the good fortune, first of all, of marrying a wonderful woman. It was love at first sight, although it took me a while to admit it—you know, male ego. Callie's patience and her tolerance of and confidence in me have given me the room to grow in my role as a husband and father. Also, my own father was a poor and uneducated Irish immigrant who taught me about loyalty, perseverance, and the value of family.

To me, the single most disturbing trend affecting our society today is the absence of fathers. That doesn't just mean physical absence due to death or divorce. It also includes the emotional absence due to a preoccupation with individual fulfillment, whether it be work or play. This absence has been linked to a number of troubling cultural changes that have been observed over the past thirty years. Let me share some of the facts:

- Today 30 percent of children are born out of wedlock, double the rate in 1970.

- By age twenty, 40 percent of girls have been pregnant at least once. About half of teen pregnancies end in birth; the other half are either miscarried or aborted.

- Almost half of all marriages end in divorce.

- The leading cause of death among teenagers aged fifteen to nineteen is suicide.

- Three out of four teen suicides occur in households where a parent has been absent, usually the father.

- Five out of six adolescents caught up in the criminal justice system come from families in which a parent, usually the father, has been absent.

I believe that fathers are essential to raising children. We can't be absent. What we provide in the home is unique and irreplaceable. Yet the role of the father continues to diminish. Today we're often seen as an older playmate, a physical education instructor, or even a second mom. Now, this stuff may be fun but it's not essential to raising kids with character.

Unfortunately many of us today are unaware that this diminished role is having a negative impact on our kids. But the fact is, many children are growing up out of balance—

immature, self-centered, irreligious, and preoccupied with material things. They may grow to be very capable and successful business people. But their personal lives are troubled.

So what's the role of a father? First of all, dads need to support and protect their kids and lead them, by example and teaching, to strength of character. That's a father's role. We need to be a living example of firm character and conscience. Kids need to respect us deeply for our strength of character, not for our own benefit but for theirs. And perhaps the most important way we earn this respect is by leading our children to honor mom. We need to put the woman we've married on a pedestal and worship her and insist on that level of respect from our kids. The children's respect for their parents and themselves begins with the parents' respect for each other.

Just four other tidbits of wisdom:

1. Think long term. Think about raising adults, not kids.

2. Talk to your kids about yourself and your friends and what you admire in them. My kids love it when Callie and I talk about our courtship.

3. Listen to your kids and praise them for their growth in character, showing them that you expect them to grow up to become great honorable men and women, regardless of what they do for a living.

4. Pass on your faith—one of the most important responsibilities we have as parents. Things don't last. But our children's souls are immortal, so there

is a lot at stake. Also, if we don't do this job well, our religious faith can disappear in a single generation. I mean, who will do this if we don't?

If you don't remember anything else about what I've said, remember this: it's especially important as fathers to recognize that the relationship we have with our children will shape the relationship they have with God. If your relationship with them is distant, remote, and disconnected, it will be difficult for them to develop a different relationship with God, their Father. If, however, it's open, loving, and close—you've set the stage for them to achieve that same kind of filial relationship with God. And that will get them to heaven.

*Philip McGovern is chief financial officer of the Heights School. He and his wife Callie have four children: Philip (PJ), Sean, Ellen, and Grace.*

# A Sense of Humor

*Paul Kamenar*

I grew up in a small town in northeastern Ohio. My father expected the best from me and my six brothers and sisters. My mother even thought I might become a priest. But this talk is as close as I'll come to that!

Neither of my parents attended college; their parents were immigrants from Hungary. They gave me and my siblings a traditional Catholic upbringing. I worked my way through college and law school. I have a sister who is a neurologist, and there's a couple of accountants in the family, a landscape architect, and so on. I was proud of my father, although his job as a real estate salesman prevented him from sharing as much time with us as we would have liked. He passed away almost twenty years ago, shortly after I graduated from law school.

My dad ushered in church on Sundays and was a member of the Knights of Columbus. But I think what impressed me most about him when I was growing up was that, whenever I would meet an adult who knew my father, he would say, "Oh, so you're Frank's boy," and then the person would go on and on, telling me what a fine person my father was. I was very proud of him.

Well, God had a different vocation for me than the one my mother may have hoped for. I married a wonderful woman, Sue, who surprised me one day when she simply gave me the book *Fatherhood* by Bill Cosby, and the great news that I was to be a father. God had certainly blessed us, and the months quickly passed when our first of two daughters was born in January 1986.

Our daughter Susan was a great joy in our lives, but also a challenge right from the beginning, not wanting to take baths or have her diapers changed. Bill Cosby's humorous book did not prepare me for this. This was no laughing matter! This was clearly on-the-job training. What Erma Bombeck said of life could be said of parenthood: "It's like a bowl of bing cherries—rich, sweet, and sometimes the pits." It has also been said—and this probably applies more to parents with teenagers—that "insanity is an inherited disease; you get it from your children!"

Three years after Susan was born, we were blessed again with our second daughter, Alice, who seemed to roll with the punches more. Or more probably, she sensed that, as parents, we were a little more relaxed about parenting.

I thoroughly enjoy being a father, helping the girls with their homework, teaching them a song or two on the piano, cheering them on at soccer games. But my job as a father has been made a lot easier since the time Sue took a leave of absence from her job as an economist at the Treasury Department when Susan was born, and never went back. As a full-time mom, homemaker, chauffeur, lunch-duty aide, fundraiser for the school, and so on, she sees the girls much more than I do, and in the evening she shares with me the delightful and sometimes not-so-delightful stories about what they did that day.

Only Sue knows everything there is to know about our girls. I recognized this very quickly when she had to go out of town for a few days to be with her mother, who was recovering from major surgery, leaving me alone to be both dad and Mr. Mom.

While I was getting the girls ready for school and making them breakfast, I gave Alice her French toast. (Knowing my culinary talents, Sue had wisely cooked them up in quantity ahead of time.) I started to pour the syrup on the French toast when Alice interrupted: "Dad, you're supposed to cut it first *before* you put the syrup on, like Mom does." "Sorry!" I said. After cutting the French toast, I thought I was finished with pouring the syrup when Alice again reminded me, "Dad, you're supposed to put the syrup on *all* the pieces— you missed a few."

Then there was the time Susan got hit in the eye by a softball at practice. After several ice-packs and a visit to the emergency room, she was recovering in her room when I brought her the most fragrant flowers from the backyard to cheer her up, only to be reminded, "Thanks, Dad, they smell great, but remember—I've got allergies."

But then there are those rare times when they say something that really drives home what the true mission of fathers is supposed to be. Alice once saw me working hard on a project—digging up part of the yard to lay down heavy slate stones for a path to the driveway—a long overdue project, as Sue will attest. Alice walked by and said to me, "Dad, you're

Christlike." I did a double-take, thinking she may have violated the Second Commandment. "What did you say?" I asked. She repeated her simple statement—"You're Christlike." At first I thought to myself that Sister Marietta certainly did a good job teaching Alice about the Fourth Commandment; or maybe Alice erroneously thought Jesus was a stone mason instead of the son of a carpenter. Then I realized that what she saw was simply a father working hard and in a loving and quiet way for his family as Christ did for us.

More important than good grades or trophies, of course, is teaching our children a love of God, a love of our faith, and a love of family. I'd like to share with you just a few tips on doing this that I find useful.

1. Catch them doing good and praise them. It takes five or six positive statements to overcome the adverse effects of a negative statement.

2. Let them know you love them, and let them know that your love is unconditional.

3. Remember that discipline is important. But as the epistle writer Paul tells us fathers, "Do not provoke your children to anger, but bring them up in the discipline and instruction of the Lord" (Eph 6:4). Set clear boundaries. When you do that, you are actually giving more freedom to your children because they know what the limits are. For example, by telling them to play only in the back yard, they know that the street is off limits. They can then enjoy their freedom without worrying whether

they're allowed to venture off. Older children need to have a definite curfew. Obviously, telling your teenager to be home by a certain time is better than telling them, "Don't stay out too late." Let them know that there are consequences for both their good and bad behavior, and while it's hard to impose the consequences when they misbehave, try to be consistent in giving the consequence.

4. Set an example. Values are usually "caught" rather than "taught."

5. Give them your *time*. We busy fathers know that our time is important, and our children know that, too— that's why they want it so much. It is sad to know that there are too many families where the father has physically abandoned his children; but if we as fathers don't spend enough time with our children— to talk to them, pray with them—we're also abandoning them emotionally. Our children grow up too quickly and we can't get those years back. Remember, no one ever said on their death bed, "Gee, I wish I would have spent more time in the office."

6. Finally, keep a good sense of humor. You'll need it!

*Paul Kamenar is Senior Executive Counsel of the Washington Legal Foundation and has argued before the U.S. Supreme Court. He also teaches at George Mason University School of Law. He and his wife Sue have two girls, Susan and Alice.*

# Crisis?
# Let God Take Over

*Michael F. Curtin*

A story is told of the pastor who was addressing the parish council at the closing meeting of the year. "Where to begin? Where to begin?" were the first words the pastor uttered. Almost immediately a voice was heard from the assembly: "As close to the end as possible, please." I will try to follow the spirit of that admonition.

What I really follow is the spirit of St. Luke, a physician, because he is tied to one of my most significant memories of being a father.

My partner in life, Kathleen, was the Director of Religious Education in our parish. We have been blessed with five children. The first four trips to Georgetown University Hospital were as seemingly pristine as St. Luke's nativity narrative. The young mother's time had come, her term was full, the baby was born, and there he or she was wrapped in swaddling clothes.

But in 1979, nine years after my youngest daughter's birth, my youngest son was about to be born. The world was now changed. Medicine was now changed. The birthing process was now changed. I was invited into the labor and delivery rooms to experience the birth of my fifth child.

Being older than most of the fathers of soon-to-be-born children, I was a bit nervous about this invitation, this change in process. Nonetheless, I wished to be a modern father, so I accepted the invitation.

Wow!!! For the first time, I saw and felt some of the agony and ecstasy of the birthing process. I saw my young son emerging into the world. I waited for his cry—and I cried. I observed Kathleen, having just gone through this horrific physical experience, now gently holding our new son. After all of the commotion subsided, I was assisted, weak-kneed, out of the birthing room.

Some weeks later, at our family retreat at Camp Maria, I found myself in the presence of our good friend and retreat master Father Gene Lenahan, who was extolling the virtues of St. Luke, the physician, and his nativity narrative. The baby is born and there he is in swaddling clothes. I piped up, "Our friend Luke may have been a physician, but he certainly wasn't an obstetrician."

Many of us are blessed to be fathers, and all of us have an idea of fatherhood. Most of us know or have known, love or have loved, fathers.

Who are some of the great fathers of both fact and fiction? As a lawyer myself, I find Atticus Finch's example to his son Jem in *To Kill A Mockingbird* etched in my mind; Finch does the job he must do, and he does it justly. Spencer Tracy's struggle with what would be best for his beautiful daughter in the movie *Guess Who's Coming to Dinner* is as real as any real-life father/daughter confrontation over interracial relationships. As that story unfolded, Spencer Tracy's character was stubbornly biased. But with pastoral nudging from a priest friend, he finally was able to understand and then bless the decision of his daughter.

On June 22, we celebrate the witness of St. Thomas More's life as a lawyer, as a Christian, and as a father. Who will ever forget the scene from the movie *A Man for All Seasons* when More explains to his daughter, Meg, the rationale for his decision to await death at the hand of his king? The quiet yet direct and unwavering example of virtue he gave to his daughter on a matter of faith and morals speaks reams about fatherhood.

And, of course, there was Robert Young in the television show *Father Knows Best*. Admittedly soapy, silly, and sophomoric, nonetheless Robert Young's character was a good and decent man who cared for the needs and happiness of his family. In today's era of shared responsibility, Robert Young's character is outdated. But the *way* he was a father is still quite illustrative and relevant.

Let me focus on a picture of great fathers not developed on the stage or screen but in real life. My father, a tough and sometimes cold person, had an immense work ethic. He was a man who accepted his responsibility as a father and did as well as he could to provide for his family.

Joseph Cardinal Bernardin, in his book of personal reflections, *The Gift of Peace,* wrote about his immigrant father:

> My father had recently undergone cancer-related surgery on his left shoulder and he was wearing a bandage under a white, short-sleeved shirt. I was

sitting on a metal railing on the porch of our friend's home, when suddenly I fell backwards, hit the ground and started crying. My father immediately jumped over the rail and picked me up. As he held me in his arms, I could see blood soaking through his shirt. He paid no attention to himself. All he wanted was to be sure I was all right. My father's ability to transcend his own illness and share in the joy of his family and friends now inspires me to try to do the same.*

What makes *my* being a father so special? It's clear that the highs about a father's role come from seeing your children well and happy. No doubt we fathers certainly like to see our children shine, no matter what the endeavor. It's natural. Strangely though, events that are strongest in my mind and memory are the events of momentary crisis, a potential or actual separation. It is the actual loss or potential for loss of the bond between father and child—child and father—that gives strength and vitality to this great gift of fatherhood. It is the instant fear that grips you when the undertow at Bethany Beach separates you from your small child even for a few seconds. It is the walk away from the airline gate, having just said goodbye to an adult child who is going to a distant land for months or perhaps years. It is the uncertainty we sense in talking with physicians about a child's debilitating or life-threatening illness. It is the pain many of us have felt when word reaches us that our father has died.

---

*Joseph Cardinal Bernadin, *The Gift of Peace: Personal Reflections* (Chicago: Loyola Press, 1997), 62.

To combat those events of separation or threatened separation, we as a people have been steeled or schooled in a faith that encourages us to let go and to let God take over.

*Michael F. Curtin, a Washington lawyer, and his wife Kathleen have five children—Michael Jr., Kevin, Christine, Colleen, and Matthew—and eight grandchildren.*

# More with Praise

## *Arthur Burnett*

What can I say to a young father in his twenties on how to raise a son or daughter today in our complex society? Or how to instill religious values? How to balance the time a father must invest in his children with the competing demands of a profession, career, or job? How to counter the negative influences of rap music, bad television, and a society awash in illegal drugs, excessive use of alcohol, and the pressures to engage in teenage and premarital sex?

From the beginning my wife and I had the philosophy that the best way to keep a child from straying was to have an agenda for each child that included extracurricular activities that developed and stimulated each child's interest and promoted his or her growth as an individual.

By 1972 we had five busy children, and there were many times we felt as if we needed to be two sets of parents. Our weekends were so busy that each of us would go to a part of one child's activity and then to the remaining activity of another child. The fifth child was still young enough to accompany one parent or the other at that stage in our lives. Thank God for car pools! Many weekends my first sit-down meal was at the end of the day.

During the week I often left work at the end of the day and went directly to a child's activity or to meetings for the

Home and School Association, a foundation, or a fundraising event, and had my dinner at 8, 9, or 10 p.m. While the children were in the lower grades, when I did come directly home from work, immediately after dinner I would spend an hour or two reviewing the day's school work with one child at a time, or preparing a child for a test the next day.

My wife and I helped our children to deliver newspapers. We helped them to participate in community-service projects. I helped the girls to sell Girl Scout cookies. I recall vividly working with my sons in their efforts to learn what was necessary to earn Cub and Boy Scout merit badges. When I ran up and down the field as a football referee, frequently being knocked down more than the players, this built a sharing approach between father and sons. Our children learned from seeing us work with them. Father-child mutual participation and partnership are far more important than merely telling a son or daughter what he or she should do.

But father-child relationships do not develop and flourish in a vacuum. Ours grew in a parish and religious community in which many others shared their religious values and made substantial commitments of their time and energies.

It has always been my philosophy that you can motivate and inspire a youngster more with praise and encouragement than you can with criticism and fault-finding. The child will reach for even greater heights and achievements in his or her personal conduct and in the activity in which he or she is engaged. Indeed, we are admonished "Fathers, do not provoke your children, or they may lose heart" (Col 3:21).

Fathers must also relate to daughters so that they will understand and appreciate boys as they grow up and later understand and appreciate men so that they can have meaningful and positive relationships and achieve a holy marriage.

Note Matthew 7:9–10: "Is there anyone among you who, if your child asks for bread, will give a stone? Or if the child asks for a fish, will give a snake?" In today's context, what does this mean? Being a father, or a mother, requires far more than being the biological parent and providing simply food and shelter. When a child needs a parent's time, guidance, and value reinforcement, the parent must be there. If you are always too busy, your child drifts, learning his or her values from television, from other individuals, or from bad influences in the community.

Fathers must teach their children to love truth and to be just. We are told: "The father of the righteous will greatly rejoice; he who begets a wise son will be glad in him" (Prov 23:24). But to achieve this holy state of joy, there must be substantial investment of time, energy, guidance, and attention to develop a "Christlike," quality person.

In hindsight, I can now say that perhaps I did not invest all the time I should have in the tug and pull of competing obligations of profession and family. Perhaps many of us reach that conclusion in later life, for children grow up, perhaps too quickly, and we wish we had had the time to do this, that, or the other thing, or that if we had, the results would have been far better and more rewarding.

On the other hand, the results haven't been too bad: we number among our children a lawyer, doctor, public-health educator, executive with Ford Motor Company, and veterinarian.

In conclusion, I note that we frequently refer to children as "my" or "our" children as if they were our "possessions"—some would say our most cherished possessions. But no, they are not material objects to possess. They are what, then? They are our replacements as we move through our short life span here on earth. They are God's children. They are the most precious of all there is on earth.

*A 1991 recipient of the Papal Medal,* **Arthur Burnett** *is a senior judge in the Washington, D.C., Superior Court and a judge-in-residence to the Children's Defense Fund concerning juvenile delinquency. He and his wife Ann a former registered nurse, have five children: Darnellena, Arthur II, Darryl, Darlisa, and Dionne.*

# Just Be There

*John R. Dugan*

### I

The parish first called me in 1989 about addressing the topic of fatherhood in public. I mentioned that my wife and I were in the midst of a divorce. I didn't receive a call back until nine years later.

Gathering my thoughts in my office, I noticed a framed Christmas card from my son Joe that simply says, "Thank you, Dad, for being there." It was obviously divine inspiration. For though my former wife and I no longer live together, we try to be there for our children at every possible moment.

Colbert King, in a *Washington Post* column entitled "The Best of Fathers," wrote: "My dad's life refuted the notion that wealth, academic degrees or social status have anything to do with being a good father. His lasting achievement was to show, through example, that the most vital and irreplaceable condition for being a good father is simply being there." About his mother, King said, "She was—and remains—a spark plug, but my father supplied the horsepower."

This is an apt description of our family, with Mary Kate, the mother of six children, being the spark plug for all of us to get in motion. In addition, I must confess she provides a lot of the horsepower to keep our family moving. She is also the heart and soul of the family. I clearly know whose opinion matters to the children. When one of them called or spoke to me, inevitably he or she asked, "Can I please speak to Mom *now?*"

Our friend Judy O'Hara has said that as a mother she has experienced feelings on "both sides of the heart"—pain and joy. She does not dwell on her very real and painful loss of a son, but on the solace of our community. In fact, the best way to learn how to be a good parent may be to look at families sitting next to you in church, at school functions, and at social gatherings. We learn from simple example.

## II

In the summer of 1951, my father died at age forty-one. I was eight years old. My mother had to take on the role of being both a father and a mother, and she returned to work as a nurse at Suburban Hospital in Bethesda, Maryland.

My father's influence on my life was significant despite the short time I had with him. He was an Army surgeon when I was born, and he missed many of my earliest years. He was a hard-working man who was driven to be the best at whatever he did. Despite his early success as a doctor, he noticed, several years before he died, that his right hand was becoming weakened from a childhood exposure to polio. He felt if he couldn't be a surgeon, he wanted to be a lawyer. On top of his busy medical practice, he attended law school at night at Catholic University. When I later entered law school myself, I thought of him often because I frequently used his *Black's Law Dictionary* in my basement study room.

Dad's sudden and early death substantially altered the Dugan family. Our lives probably would have been easier had he lived. It certainly pushed me sooner toward adulthood and required me to become more self-reliant than I otherwise might have been.

As I noted above, my mother had to become "father" and bread-winner. She worked very hard, not only at Suburban Hospital, but in doctors' offices and later as a private duty nurse. For the last eight or nine years of her practice, she often had night duty, leaving our home in Silver Spring at 10:30 in the evening and returning before we awakened in the morning. She was an excellent provider and was able to educate my older brother, Tee, and younger sister, Mary Ann, by sending us to private high schools: St. John's, Gonzaga, and Immaculata. All three of us thereafter graduated from college, and each of us attained a professional degree. She also paid off the mortgage on a nurse's salary.

Mother had help in her role as a dual parent from her four brothers, who at various times and in different ways became "our four fathers." Uncles Bill, Joe, Jack, and Jim McDevitt were always there for us children, attending our games and school events, and providing us examples of the manly virtues of being there for one's children or, in this case, one's nephews and niece.

We were also blessed to have an older male neighborhood friend who become our mentor: Reverend Joe Kleinstuber, or Father "K." At the time of my father's death, he was in graduate school trying to get into medical school. He often would play basketball with us or just be there for us. He coached us at Our Lady of Lourdes, became a U.S. Air Force officer, and later entered the seminary to become a priest. As our family priest, he married Mary Kate and me and baptized each of our six children.

It is commonly thought by non-Catholics, and not a few Catholics, that priests cannot offer advice on marriage or parenthood because they have never been married and have no children. Nonsense. Recently, I was honored to give a eulogy at the funeral mass for Reverend John Bellwoar, who taught me at Gonzaga. I began: "When I read the obituary column, I was struck by the last paragraph: 'He leaves no immediate survivors.' While technically accurate, it is not true. There are thousands of 'survivors' of Father John Bellwoar, and I am proud to proclaim I am one of them. I was one of his pupils, one of his penitents, one of his friends."

The wisdom of priests helps us become better parents. Father D'Silva was the first in our parish to transpose "brothers and sisters in Christ" to its proper sequence, "sisters and brothers in Christ." By this small but important gesture, he heightened our awareness of the primacy of women in our lives.

Monsignor Duffy's homilies are full of references to a wide variety of books and articles that he has recently read that inform him on all sorts of matters, including parenthood. (Incidentally, I know of only one other person who is as widely read as Father Duffy—my dear friend, Gonzaga High School classmate, and fellow parishioner Bill Bennett.)

Stories matter. Stories from the Bible and literature, as well as from people who share their experiences as mothers

and fathers, or as priests who counsel fathers and mothers—
these stories make a difference in our lives.

### III

The most important thing I have ever done is to have
fathered our children and nurtured their growth and development. Everything else pales in comparison.

I seek no reward for this God-given opportunity and
duty other than a simple thanks from my family for "being
there." While there have been difficult times in my life, I have
always trusted that *he* will "be there for me." *He* has given
me the strength and wisdom to overcome some of the
crosses. As a result of his grace, I have always looked on life
as "a glass half full rather than half empty."

Early years with children contain very special memories.
We have recorded them in home color sound movies that I
keep in my bedroom and perennially promise to convert to
videotapes. I never seem to have enough money or time to do
this. It is certainly one of my lifelong goals.

I have switched to snapshot picture taking. Other
fathers and mothers get a kick out of me and have said that
I have a camera attached to my hands at all times. I try to
record many happy events that we share with our children,
such as family dinners, school events, and parties with my
children's friends. I order an extra set of prints in case any of
my friends wish to see their children pictured with one or
more of my own.

In a file I keep of impressive pieces from the newspaper,
I came across a column by Richard Cohen entitled, "At 80,

He Has to Explain Nothing." Cohen was commenting about his father on the occasion of his eightieth birthday:

> My father is not a great man and leaves no public record of his accomplishments. He has written no book, built no building, accumulated no real wealth....You tell me what greatness is. You tell me if to be good for 80 years, to be both moral and ethical, is not greatness....You tell me if a man who has never cheated in business or love, who seemed always to tell the truth and who abjured bitterness is not great. It seems to me he is.

Cohen's description of his father sounds a lot like how I hope to be remembered.

We do not have to wait until our eightieth birthday to receive feedback on the kind of job we are doing. I hope that I will not slight any of my children by mentioning only two examples. My oldest son, John, was graduating from Trinity College. As we were awaiting the parade of graduates, I learned he had received an award for poetry. I read for the first time "A Poem for My Father." In it, he brought together many experiences in my life, including a telephone call I received late one evening from him while he was enjoying a spring term in Rome. It was four in the morning in Italy. He wrote:

> Tonight I remember how I cried in Rome, in the quiet of that four in the morning piazza, water spilling in the fountain behind me. I was overcome

by sentiment, overcome because you never had that opportunity.

When I called you, demanding that you visit me, you said that it was enough just knowing that I was in Rome. I know you meant that, Dad. Even though you couldn't afford the trip, you meant that you've always found real happiness in your children. That is your gift, a gift I want.

The second example of positive feedback relates to my daughters. The teenage and young-adult years with our children are rich with pluses and minuses. I have especially enjoyed the opportunity to take the older children to visit prep schools and colleges. Applying to colleges is a time-consuming and difficult process. It has at times strained our relationship. Nevertheless, I recall how proud I was to listen to admissions officers comment on the strength of our daughters, Christina and Katherine. Our daughters did not have multiple sports awards to supplement their academic achievements, but these officers said they are good and decent young ladies and we want them. Quite a reward to a father and mother.

## IV

While I realize I have touched upon some very personal aspects of my life, I have done so to help others who have had to deal with a divorce or early death of a parent. God has given our family strength and courage to face changes. We simply have to deal with whatever comes to us in life and trust in God that he has and will "be there for us."

Finally, on a lighter note, I want to share the wisdom of my son David, who once dutifully listened to me talk about the loss of my father and the fact that one never knows if God will call one sooner rather than later. There was a silence at the dinner table, then David stated, "If that happens, Dad, don't worry. I've got first dibs on your bedroom."

*John R. Dugan is a trial lawyer practicing in Washington, D.C., and in Maryland. He and his former wife, Mary Kate, have six children: John Jr., Joseph, Katherine, Christina, David, and Matthew.*

# Omnipresence

## *George Peacock*

I ran across a quote of late that touches on a hazard of fatherhood: "I want to die in my sleep like my grandfather... not yelling and screaming like the passengers in his car."

Father's Day was formalized as a national holiday only in 1966. In contrast, Mother's Day celebrations can be traced back to the spring celebrations of ancient Greece. Fathers, I think we know where we stand.

I never really think about Father's Day presents. That's because my son, Duncan, was born on Father's Day, and nothing could ever compare to that except, perhaps, the new Internet-enabled Palm VII, at $599 at Best Buy. They're open on Sunday.

In honor of the Trinity and the Jesuits who taught me, I think there is a tripartite life cycle to being a father. We men all start out as sons. If we're lucky enough, that's where we learn about unconditional love. I was particularly lucky because I had two great parents who shepherded seven of us—six boys and a girl.

One of the main things I remember about growing up was that my dad seemed to be at everything I ever did. He coached every single one of us in Little League. He got up at five each morning to help with our morning paper routes. He was at my basketball games, baseball games, and track meets (in or out of town); he was at school plays and musicals. He always seemed to make the time to be there, even though there were seven of us to attend to. When my sister Anne was playing basketball at Yale, he was known to drive six hours from Rochester, watch her game, and then drive home. How my parents achieved such omnipresence with seven children is beyond me. That's one of my main goals as a father— omnipresence. I want to be there.

To understand stage two in the tripartite life cycle, one must go back to the Garden of Eden and the first son, Adam. God loved Adam as most of our parents loved all of us— unconditionally. And it was good, too good, maybe. It is only with sorrow that we know true joy. It is only through sin that we can experience redemption. Without bad, we cannot choose the good. And so God gave us woman that men might come to know all their imperfections. Thus my gift idea for wives on Father's Day is this: pretend that your husband doesn't have faults. You remember that, don't you? You've done it before. It's called "dating."

Finally, in stage three, the cycle repeats itself and we become fathers ourselves, with children whom we love unconditionally and who, at least for a while, love us unconditionally in return.

It is said that children are the gifts we give to a time that we will never see. These days, there seems to be a great focus on genealogy, the roots that shape us. More often, I wonder about who is next and what I can do to shape them. As Kahlil Gibran wrote, "If the grandfather of the grandfather of Jesus had known what was hidden within him, he would have stood humble and awe-struck before his soul."

Who is coming after you? What are you doing to make them better?

Finally, I'd like to acknowledge our alma paters. We call our schools our alma maters, but it is our priests who are our nourishing, loving, "other fathers." They prepare our parents before we are even born, and they welcome us into the Church. For many of us, they are there as we grow in knowledge and faith; they are there when we marry, when we are sick, and when we die.

As we sat in Mass a few months ago, my daughter Hayley turned to me and said, "Daddy, I really like Father D'Silva. You know, he's nicer than Jesus!" Now isn't that a challenge?

*George Peacock is an expert in corporate executive benefits. His wife Stacy Murchison Peacock works in insurance and investments. They have four children: Duncan, the twins Hayley and June, and Mackenzie.*

# Up All Night

## *Don Kosin*

At birth, our daughter, Katharine, had a problem with her blood-sugar levels that caused her to be placed in a special care unit of Holy Cross Hospital the first weekend of her life. As I paced the hospital halls and drove home alone after visiting hours, I prayed as I had never prayed before, and found strength and trust in the Lord that I never would have thought was possible under the circumstances. I became closer to God that weekend in March 1988 than I had in the thirty years before.

I was blessed with the opportunity to spend Katharine's first twenty-one days home with her and my wife. Every day seemed a new miracle. During that twenty-one-day period of watching Katharine during all her waking hours, I first began to get insights, through my relationship with her, into our relationship with God. It is no coincidence that when we make the sign of the cross, we refer to "the Father." Only after being a parent have I come to fully appreciate the image of God as our father. This image helps us to understand how we relate to God and what God's love means. As a parent, I have increasingly found that when my daughter is happy or delighted, it delights me. When she is upset or disappointed, it upsets me. I share her joy and her pain in a way I never thought possible. This helps me understand how and why

God wants us to be happy and shares our joy when we are. It also helps me understand what a supreme sacrifice it was for God to see his Son suffer and die on the cross to save us.

Of course, as parents, we know that while giving children whatever they want may make them smile in the short run, it is not truly in their best interests. I can now better understand how God the Father must feel when he sees us act in a way that is not truly in our interests, and how loving it is when God, acting through the Holy Spirit, rebukes us when we do so. Perhaps most importantly, being a parent helps me understand how God can still love us and forgive us even when we act in a way that is hurtful. Finally, being a parent helps me to understand how our indifference to God—the times we may simply seem to forget he is there—are even worse than moments of anger or even resentment. I know it hurts me more to have my daughter ignore me than to be angry at me or even rude to me. That helps me to understand that I must remain aware of God and constantly nurture my relationship with him.

Ironically, the night I was asked to speak about fatherhood, Katharine was up all night sick. It occurred to me as we were tending to her through the night, knowing that I had to get up and teach a first-grade Sunday-school class the next morning, that a parent's love means making sacrifices, without a moment's thought, that would have seemed an undue burden before becoming a parent. It's like the Boy's Town slogan, "He ain't heavy, he's my brother." When there is the slightest sense that your child is in distress or discomfort, there is not a thought of how unpleasant it may be to go without sleep or to clean a dirty diaper or the contents of an upset stomach.

I'd like to end with a final note on fatherhood vs. parenthood. My wife and I have had an arrangement in place since she returned to work when Katharine was four months old. I recommend it to all working couples, at least those with only one child. Since July 1988, every day—both weekday and weekend—either my wife or I assume primary responsibility for Katharine. This has meant changing diapers, feeding, waking up at night, sitting through animated films in movie theaters, and running next to her bike to catch her when she falls. The other parent gets to be a "grandparent," engaging Katharine only to the extent he or she wants. Of course, Katherine has always seemed to seek out the parent who is due the "night off."

It requires some horse-trading and juggling of days and hours, and it's tricky when we are sick, but it has ensured equality of sorts in responsibility. One might hypothesize that, with both parents working the same hours and sharing the same responsibility, each of us would be more a "parent" than playing distinct "mother" and "father" roles. I am here to say that this hypothesis would be incorrect. When Katharine is truly sick or in distress, she still insists on mommy. I luck out as the one she seems to want to be with when she wants to play and frolic. It gives me an excuse to be a little kid again, another great advantage of fatherhood!

*Don Kosin is an attorney for the Medicare program. He and his wife Joyce Somsak have a daughter Katharine.*

# You Cannot Love Too Much

## *John J. Gorman*

The way in which it was arranged for me to be up here this morning speaks volumes about my role as father and husband in the Gorman household. I have always wondered about how and why people would get up in front of the congregation and talk about very personal aspects of their marriage and family. Not me, of course!

Well, the telephone rang one Saturday morning and my wife answered it. I heard, "Hello, Father Percy." The next thing that I heard was, "He would be delighted to...but let me just check to make sure that he is in town that Sunday."

Well, here I am, giving one of those dreaded personal-type talks. And the only thing I am absolutely sure of is that my teenage daughter is *soooo* glad, counting-her-blessings glad, to be out of town at this very moment so that she does not have to suffer the extreme embarrassment I would undoubtedly cause her by talking in public. And I assure you, from an embarrassment standpoint, that it wouldn't matter what I had to say.

Fathers with teenage daughters may know what I am talking about, but it seems to me that there are two primary, and unpredictably fluctuating, stages of the father/teenage daughter relationship. I am either the loving, want-to-hold-your-hand, put-my-arm-around-you father, or the "Dad, stop that, you're embarrassing me" one.

I have one interesting observation about this past week reflecting on what I would share with my fellow fathers. It turns out that both my wife and daughter, the girls in our household, have been out of town together—out of the country, in fact—for the past ten days. And I have noticed that, with just the two boys in the house, there seems to have been just a little more opportunity for contemplative quietude than normal. I will not go down that road any further.

One result of my week of reflection has been the belated realization of how fortunate I am to be a father. It is truly a gift from God, I am grateful and thankful to God for it, and I think that all of us fathers should be. I know that I have taken that great gift for granted. I have more than one good friend who is married and childless, but not by choice, who would give up any possession to be able to have children. (Of course, there have been times that I have offered to give them one of mine!)

There have been no greater joys in my life than those I realize almost on a daily basis with my children: whether it is the "I love you, Dad" as a telephone conversation ends, or after prayers and goodnights are said, or whether it is one of those priceless and unique expressions that emanate from the pure innocence and thought process of a child. For example, there's the five-year-old's question: "Is it today yet?" I only wish I had jotted them all down as they came out over the years.

Let's not forget why there is a Father's Day in the first place (putting aside the Hallmark-, Old Spice-, and Sears-led corporate-greed conspiracies). There is a day of recognition for fathers because fatherhood is hard work to do it right.

Also, being a father is a life-long task. I remember the line by Jason Robards in Steve Martin's movie *Parenthood*—"It's not like it ends when they leave your house. They are always your children."

There is no adequate go-to, game book, or manual on being a father and raising children. A famous Hollywood screenwriter is reported to have said, "In spite of all the experience that Hollywood people have in making movies, nobody knows anything." I sometimes think that the same statement is true of being a father and raising children. Early on in fatherhood, it is only the mother-in-law who knows all the answers.

My "manual" more often than not has been my wife, and when the kids approach and the requests start—"Dad, can I...Dad, can we?"—I quickly pipe in, "What did your mom say?" And if the answer comes back, "She said to ask you," then I know that I have a tough decision to make.

It seems to me that there is only one rule of fatherhood that can be followed without error. And it is basically the Golden Rule (I don't mean, he who has the gold rules). It seems to me that you cannot love your children too much. You can over- and under-discipline them, you can be too lax or buy them too much, but you cannot give them too many hugs and too much love.

To take a little of the pressure off, with respect to any other fatherhood decision you have to make, just keep in mind that whatever you decide, you have a fifty-fifty chance of being right.

With my youngest being an eight-year-old, the infant-baby-toddler years of being a father are behind me (or at least I hope they are). I have moved into the arena of sleep-overs, homework, dances, and the never-ending sporting events. With three children now registered in at least one organized sport each season, it is impossible to be everywhere at the same time for all three games every Saturday and Sunday. It is for this reason that I have arranged to have my parents move to nearby Bethesda from South Carolina. We needed one more screaming fan in attendance than my wife and I could muster.

My years of fatherhood have now moved beyond American Girl dolls, Ninja Turtles, and Pokémon cards to lacrosse sticks, stereos and CD players, Abercrombie and Fitch, and the Limited II. Just around the corner lies college tuition, the real motivation to keep those kids playing sports. I figure that a scholarship of any sort would be the equivalent of winning the lottery and not having to pay taxes.

God bless all the children, whoever they may be, which my eight-year-old would remind me means everyone, because every person is a child of someone.

*John J. Gorman, an attorney, and his wife Susan, a former attorney, have three children: Katherine, Charlie, and Will.*

# The Heart of the Matter

## *Peter Ross*

I'm not one of the prominent journalists, politicians, or other Washington heavyweights who attend Mass at Blessed Sacrament. The reason my name might ring a bell, however, is that for some time now you have prayed for me.

People have petitioned God on my behalf for almost one hundred weeks. If anyone fears that petitioning might become too rote, I gain strength and hope each time I hear my name. I believe the power of prayer has worked to keep me *on* the list of the sick and *off* the list that follows it. So I am full of thanks.

How did I find myself in need of such prayer? On a perfect July Saturday morning, my longtime tennis partner and I were heading to the Edgemoor Club courts. There was a man on Court Two whom I did not recognize; he turned out to be a cardiologist. We would meet in minutes.

As my friend and I warmed up, I felt clammy, almost nauseous. I couldn't get comfortable, even after lying down. What was happening? It can't be my heart, I pleaded to myself. I had never had heart trouble. Work had been crazy for some time, but there had been no angina, no warning signs, not a clue. As the pain in my chest grew unbearable, I realized it could be little else. Lying there, listening to the sound of my son Colin rallying on the backboard just a few feet away, I was having a heart attack.

An hour and a half later at the hospital, the pain was gone. The doctors found my system surprisingly clean, but a small bit of plaque in my main artery had somehow ruptured. The extent of the resulting heart damage also surprised them, though they thought the coming months would bring some recovery. I checked out of the hospital three days later, humbled, tremendously thankful to be alive, set to resume my old life.

That was not to be. One complication after another sent me back to the emergency room. Among other things, the heart attack had left me with an arrhythmia that could cause sudden death. So I needed a defibrillator/pacemaker. Before that procedure could be performed, they took me off the blood thinners that were protecting my artery against reclotting. That didn't turn out well. Twenty minutes after returning home from the hospital, I suffered a massive second heart attack.

I have only limited recollections of the days and weeks that followed, as I remained on a ventilator while doctors tried to keep me alive. One clear memory I do have is the reassuring presence and unwavering devotion of Father D'Silva at my side—even if I did panic a bit that he might be giving me the last rites! In a fog of fear and confusion, I had a profound awareness of many people working through prayer to pull me back.

I also remember, and think often, of one particular moment in which I felt an overwhelming sense of surrender, a sense that it was time to let go. I prayed desperately that I wanted to be there for my family, that I must be there for my children. I absolutely believe that holding fast to my love for them saved my life. I can still see the intensive care unit walls covered with gorgeous black and white photos of my kids that a close friend had taken (and stayed up all night printing). They inspired a fantastic team of doctors and nurses not to give up on this young guy with the beautiful little kids.

So many of the seemingly fundamental roles of being a father are no more. I hadn't really recognized how much my identity as a father (and as a man) had, over time, come to rely upon such traditional elements as working hard, being the breadwinner, achieving stature in my career, and having physical strength. How often I felt fathering was lifting and fixing things, showing the kids how to play sports (and being athletic myself), roughhousing with the kids, or sweeping them off their feet for a hug.

Those roles are gone for me now. My days revolve around medicines, cardiac rehab, rest, and trying to delay the need for a transplant. I no longer have the stamina to work, to earn, to find status as a successful lawyer. Now I leave all the heavy lifting—and most everything else, it seems—to my wife, Althea. Being stripped of these tools for being a dad, for being a man, is both humbling and frustrating.

Yet I try hard (if not always successfully) to focus not on what is lost, but what is left. So what *is* left to give, to teach, to model for my children? Well, what is left—more than that, what I have *gained*—are things like these:

- A sense that today, and not some tomorrow, is the day to tell my kids—and, even more, to show them—how precious they are to me and to the world;

- A heightened attention that we now pay to each child—not just to their big school events or ball-games, but also to their everyday lives;

- The unmistakable lesson that though we cannot dictate the path of our lives, we can control how we respond to what has come our way;

- The wonder that hardship draws us closer to God;

- The discovery that the strength of one's body has little to do with the strength of one's character;

- The knowledge that a sick heart can still be a joyful—even a laughing—heart;

- A deep and genuine thankfulness that we offer for the gift of life, the gift of family, and the gift of community.

These are among the things that I am still able and committed to provide to my children. Many times I am too tired, other times too eager, to do a great job of it. But, at this stage, my energies are devoted to little else.

I am left to wonder whether those other roles that I can no longer serve are really the core or only the usual trappings of fatherhood. Perhaps these things I have "fallen back" on—love, faith, character, joyfulness, thankfulness—are indeed the essence of what it is to be a father.

*Peter Ross was raised a Presbyterian in California and has attended Catholic church with his wife Althea Harlin since they first met in Cambridge, Massachusetts, in 1983. He has degrees from Stanford and Harvard Law School and for fifteen years practiced before or served at the Federal Communications Commission in Washington, D.C. He now spends his time not so much "doing" as "being" with his wife and their three children: Maddie, Colin, and Brian.*

# The Greatest Privilege

*Rick Cannon*

Fathering gathered in me, it seems, like a poem does, when that flicker of idea becomes a certainty, when everything is relevant, even at first draft. There was the brimming joy and pride of the new owner before he gets his prize home, the late-night realization that *he's* being measured by *it,* that he's put his own humanity, talent, and patience on the line; and then the real work kicked in. Like a poem, for me fathering began with a certain breezy frivolity and ended up requiring everything I had; and like all good art, it had its surprise: my children made a man of me. But here the metaphor dies: unlike the poem, fathering is entirely real; and you can't revise.

It wasn't for nearly seven years, after grad school and a term of self indulgence, that my wife, Lori, and I took out our first lease on the "baby carriage." Planning was iffy. While we agreed strategically, there were tactical differences. When I suggested, "Let's have our babies bang, bang, bang," she replied, "Let's see how I feel after the first 'bang.'" Lori, one of seven, wanted only two; I, one of four, pushed for three. We compromised at five.

We were blessed with fertility. In fact, we placed the little guys like golf shots in six quick years: Billy, Corinne, Molly, and then the double bogey of twins, John and Joe,

101

who provide the percussive backbeat to our lives even now, twenty years later, as we struggle with multiple jobs and refinancings to cover their college tuitions, the "twin bill" at the end of our list. Every birth for me was new and powerful. Like no other experience I've ever had, from spine to fingertip, each was a light, floating joy. When Billy crowned and emerged, I could barely catch my breath. The tiled delivery room, cold and bright, tilted. Another power was breathing there, elusive, but palpable, huge, and kind. For me, it was the beginning of belief. Six years later, as I drove home from the hospital after our last, a snow shower suddenly enveloped Sligo Creek Parkway. The air was gauzy with dancing flakes, my joy somehow floating over the earth.

But what, in heaven's name, had we done? Those early years, as any parent will report, were a blur of diapers, carpooling, kiddy sports, and a messy house. Did we like it? Not a relevant question. We both were in the family soup, gung-ho sailors in a gale. In ten years, we spent $10,000 on 33,000 diapers. A normal weekday involved three-to-five hours in the car. We cheered them on through twenty-five basketball seasons, an equal number of soccer seasons, and attended several dozen back-to-school nights and band concerts, while holding three or four jobs each.

We couldn't afford vacations. For many years, Lori taught triple the normal course load for a college professor and hustled a regular schedule of workshops and consulting gigs off campus; in addition to high school teaching, I taught weekends at a local college and ran a summer school. A friend of ours once joked that we had turned teaching into an Amway franchise. We'd exchange cars in the college parking lot; she'd pull in with sleeping tots in car seats to begin her teaching stint, and I'd drive them home, picking up the evening duties. Though we saw each other little in those years, I count it a singular blessing to have avoided daycare.

As father of five in six years, I had no learning curve. What I did wrong, they all suffered in equal measure, and the same with what I did right. My fathering was by reflex, tempered (in concert with Lori's saner thinking) by two principles that became a kind of mantra in our house: *be kind* and *do a good job*. Good work is the key to success in anything; the genius of genius is endurance.

It's hard to separate fathering from mothering in those early years, we were such a team. But I saw, ironically, how mothering *can* separate wife from husband. Shortly after our first was born, Lori came home from teaching to find me "in my cups," jiggling the baby on my knee, somewhat dangerously, she thought. There was a scene. In quite the manly act, I broke a chair. She was unimpressed, standing there with the baby on her hip, a firm set to her mouth. From the beginning of our marriage, she'd stood by me as I struggled with alcohol, but the way she stood there that evening was the way women stand with babies in doorways. I haven't had a drink since, twenty-six years and counting. Even now, when she's in one of those snits peculiar to women, I'll send the kids into the house ahead of me for protection.

Some variations from my own upbringing: I never spanked my children, I never told them I was disappointed in them, and I spoiled them with things. This last, I see now, was an error, though it began innocently enough, with $100 basketball shoes. My children as adults tend to live beyond their means. Speaking of errors, what ever induced me to become so spit-sputtering angry when Billy let the baby shove two cassettes into the van's player? And why one winter did I enclose that newborn mouse in a paper bag and smash it with a maul on the deck as all the children watched? Something I'm sure they'll never forget. Once I made two-year-old Joey stand outside in the backyard for a half hour because, as I explained later to Lori when the older kids ratted me out, "It was either that or kill him."

These and things like it are my fathering crimes—impatience, poor judgment, unkindnesses—at least the crimes I know of. I'm sure other events, words, ways of being that I'm too myopic to see, have burned into my children; for the father, as I well know, is a powerful agent.

My own father was a tough man. He set the bar high, and if I didn't make it, there was no lenience. In most cases, the bar was too high. I couldn't get over it, and I haven't gotten over it yet. I remember once as a fourth or fifth grader he bet me a sum of money against yard work that I couldn't leap up and touch the ceiling of our living room by his birthday. I got so I could do it most times I tried. The day he said, "Let's see," I took a jump and missed. That was it. The only jump allowed. Later in the day, I got high enough to jam my palm to the ceiling, but it didn't count. That's the way he was. No margin. I think he also wanted that free yard work.

Now, at fifty-five, having reared five children of my own, I can see him with a new perspective. He loved me, I know that. And as far as I'm concerned, that's the only thing a father absolutely has to communicate. I'm not at all sure that he liked me. That I didn't like him much strikes me as irrelevant: a father has to like his child, or at least give that impression. But the man was dedicated to us (and to his business). That's all he did. He worked with us tirelessly in sports, in speech and debate, in school projects. He got down into our lives, our friends, our problems.

We seem hard-wired to not only receive but magnify the paternal signal. I know now my father's bar was too high, his enforcement too strict, his demeanor too rigid; it still hurts. The power of the father is truly frightening. More than for the myriad things he does right, we remember him—perhaps flinch all our lives—for his errors. I don't know, for example, whether my own father was ever proud of me after I left his immediate purview. He never said so.

I hate to think of the long reach my own errors may be having in my children's lives. Many intangibles may escape our notice. For example, for years Lori spoke of this look of exasperation, disappointment, and censure that flew across my face when I was displeased, a kind of involuntary tic she said was devastating. I couldn't fathom it until I saw my own father give a withering glance to my mother when she didn't hold a flood lamp correctly as he was photographing one of our children. "That's the look," Lori said. Since then, I have tried to beat it, tried for the neutral mask no matter what is happening. She doesn't complain about it anymore, so maybe I've been successful. But have I affected my children with it? The pain of it, or, almost worse, the habit? What other subtle but damaging quirks may have gotten through?

I have always felt that there should be a little *oh sh——, here he comes* about us fathers, that we set a standard and provide consequences because the moms (at least in my mother's and Lori's cases) are such pushovers; so I think the "strong arm" role comes with the fathering territory. But I didn't want to throb in my kids' heads like a dinged thumb, so I made it a point, with a little help from Lori, to have some leniency, to have a willingness to adjust standards to "makeable" levels that fit the individual child.

Perhaps to our relief, one father is never sufficient. I've seen that in my own case, both as a son and a father; and I see it occurring constantly among my high school students. By sophomore or junior year, there's a disenchantment between father and child. Sudden differences of opinion crop up, and kids can and do get into serious trouble—bad grades, broken curfews, drinking, drugs, court appearances, sexual adventuring, car accidents. It's a minefield of event-and-control issues centered on one who no longer will be controlled in the old way; and the adolescent looks around for models other than parents. Even if there are no great disagreements, there's the yen on the youngster's part for something different. Most of us saw our dad in his daily round, got the dinner-table gist of his concerns, his seeming burial in business, his political drift—I know my children saw *me* on *my* little track—and generation to generation the response is the same: "There's got to be another way!"

I'm working on a poem about one of my other fathers who died young. A local community leader and speech coach, he died in a car accident, and it still hurts forty years after. Our real fathers, who changed our diapers, who saw us through halting first steps of the most rudimentary skills, and whose hope for us is blind, are often incapable of seeing us as peers for many years. It takes another man—a teacher, a coach, a scoutmaster, a grandfather, an older male who takes an interest—to welcome and affirm this child citizen as an intellectual and integrated young adult.

Every father is a son and, from that experience, holds the twin lights of what he admires and how he's been hurt to negotiate this fathering path. Sitting down with the little one, you loosen your tie, open your heart, and take the clock from the wall. A father finally must do only one thing: let his sons and daughters know there is nothing they can say or do to stop him from loving them. This is an anchor for their lives, a sun for their world, the prime meridian of their time here. And children give back.

My children made me grow up. They required everything I had, then opened up new territory. They gave me faith. They showed me one must step carefully in this world, that what one says, and how one says it, and what one does, and how one does it, is important and cannot be retracted. They taught me gratitude and joy and many surprising details about love. They taught me about time, money, anger management, and not to sweat the small stuff. The greatest privilege I've ever had is being their dad.

*Rick Cannon is co-editor of* Poet Lore. *His first collection of poetry,* The Composition of Absence, *was published in 2003. He has taught English to hundreds of Blessed Sacrament graduates in his twenty-seven years at Gonzaga College High School. He and his wife Lori Shpunt, who is a vice president of Trinity College, have five children: Billy, Corinne, Molly, John, and Joe.*

# Let the Little Ones Come Unto Me

*Douglas W. Kmiec*

For me, fatherhood is only comprehensible in terms of the family. The Holy Father calls family "the first vital cell of civilization." Nothing goes well in the larger culture if it is not taught well in the home first.

I am a lifelong teacher, but my children's teaching of me follows Matthew's Gospel, Chapter 18, in which Christ suffers the little children to come to him, and says that to enter heaven, we must become like them.

Take my eldest son, now twenty-four and in law school at the University of California at Berkeley. When he was six, we gave Keenan his first two-wheel bicycle. We left the new bike in the front drive for him to discover when he came home. But when he first saw it, he didn't assume it was his. Instead Keenan said sweetly: "Dad, one of the neighborhood kids must have left his bike here." In that moment, I knew our son would never be plagued by the false happiness promised by the things of this world.

When I came to Washington, D.C., to be dean at The Catholic University Law School, I was convinced that it was truly God's invitation. But our second oldest, Kate, was not able to come with us. While she is over twenty-one, out of

college, and working, it was wrenching to leave her a conti-
nent away, outside Los Angeles. Yet she knew what her
father must do, and she patiently waited, keeping a candle in
the window for our return.

Named for Judge Roger Kiley, a classmate of the Gipper
at Notre Dame, our son Kiley was about to start his senior
year of high school when I agreed to take the deanship. It
meant moving him out of Malibu High School—co-ed, unde-
manding, easy access to surf the Pacific—to Gonzaga High
School—all male, very demanding, where even surfing the
net is frowned upon. Kiley didn't flinch; he didn't even seriously complain, and with a generous heart, hugging his
father more than once, he became in the vernacular of that
fine Jesuit school "a man for others." His was a true lesson
of self-sacrifice, as the Holy Father says, of finding ourselves
by giving ourselves to others.

The twins, Kolleen and Kloe, had no choice but to tag
along with their wandering parents. They have babysat for
many children at Blessed Sacrament already, but they are
truly their own best friends, illustrating the virtue of true
friendship better than Aristotle's *Ethics*.

In return for all these gifts of innocent instruction, what
have I shared with my children? A few years back, I had
occasion to write a book called *Cease-Fire on the Family*. If
Barnes & Noble or Borders ordered more regularly from my
mother's garage, you would have heard of it. It suggested
that the way out of the culture wars was not law or politics,
but family, specifically, a family willing to pass on to their
children three core beliefs:

- First, belief in God, for without it, all of life is without purpose.

- Second, belief in a knowable truth—something the American founders easily called "self- evident."

- Third, a working knowledge of the four cardinal virtues. *Cardinal* is from the Latin *cardo,* meaning "hinge." So much of a life well lived does indeed hinge upon these: prudence (readily seeking the advice of others), justice (recognizing the inherent dignity of every created person), courage (having the capacity to maintain one's faith in a culture that denies its importance), and temperance (being moderate, as well as modest, in all things).

One last thought: Notre Dame's Father Theodore Hesburgh, who brought me into teaching many years ago, once told me, "The best thing a father can do for his children is never to stop loving their mother." It's good advice.

*Douglas W. Kmiec is Caruso Family Chair in Constitutional Law at Pepperdine University in Malibu, California. He was recently dean of the law school at The Catholic University of America. He and his wife Carol have five children: Keenan, Kate, Kiley, Kolleen, and Kloe.*

# "Ave Maria" on the CD Player

*Pat Wingert Kelly*

The birth of our first baby should have been filled with much joy for my husband, Brian, and me. The problem was our infant son came too early—way too early. Most babies are born at forty weeks. Our son, Daniel, was born at twenty-four weeks—sixteen weeks early—and weighed only one pound three ounces. If he hadn't been tethered to so many tubes and wires, I could have held him in the palm of my hand. The doctors said his prospects were extremely poor. They told us to prepare ourselves, saying there was only a five percent chance that he would survive.

Up to that point, my husband and I were like most other middle-class thirty-year-old couples. We were college-educated working people who always had been able to take care of any problem that confronted us by ourselves. We thought of ourselves as very competent, even a little invincible.

And then came Danny. Suddenly we didn't feel very invincible. In fact, we felt helpless.

Nothing prepares a new parent for the overwhelming love you feel for a new baby. All this love for him was pouring out of us, just as the doctors were warning us that he likely would slip away at any moment. We felt confused, helpless, and useless. While the doctors and nurses were busy trying to keep him alive, there was almost nothing we could do—but pray.

We started praying as we'd never prayed before. For myself, I was desperately seeking some connection to God through which I could reach him most effectively.

As I sat thinking about this, "Ave Maria" came on the CD player. I started thinking of the Blessed Virgin for the first time as a real woman, as a real mother, someone who had experienced the anguish of having her baby's life endangered. I started thinking about how she and Joseph must have felt as they fled Bethlehem in the middle of the night for Egypt after the angel warned them of Herod's plan to kill all the newborn babies in his land. In those moments, Mary became a real person to me, rather than a distant deity or figure from a nativity set. I felt that she knew exactly how I felt, and I started praying to her in a way I never had before. I prayed that she would reach out and help my baby, and if he were destined to die, that she would help us find the strength we needed.

I found great peace in those prayers and comfort in knowing that, if my baby were taken from me, he would go to heaven and be with Mary where he would be safe and happy. To me, that was the worst-case scenario. And as I prayed, I realized I could deal with that.

From the beginning, our parish also held out a comforting hand. Monsignor (Thomas) Duffy, our pastor, put Daniel on the list of the sick we prayed for at Mass and kept him there for four and a half months, until he came home from the hospital.

I will never forget being in the intensive care nursery one day and looking up to see Father Duffy praying over Daniel's incubator and blessing him. When I remarked to a nurse how touched I was by this, she seemed surprised. "Didn't you know he's been coming every Sunday since Daniel was born?" she said. I can't express the sense of gratitude I felt to him and the parish. Up to that point, Blessed Sacrament was just the place we went to church. From that point on, the parish became "our parish." The connection between our family and Blessed Sacrament became the "ties that bind."

We believe those prayers were heard. Though he had a very rough course, Danny miraculously persevered, surviving each obstacle as it came his way. The doctors and nurses started calling him "the miracle baby." After four and a half months in intensive care, we took home a comparatively hefty four-pound baby—on oxygen, on heart and lung monitors, and with a tangle of complications—but incredibly healthy considering the journey he had been on.

Since that time, the Holy Family has had a special meaning for me, and I continue to pray to Mary in a way I don't pray to anyone else.

I find myself wishing that the New Testament gave us more information about the everyday family life of Jesus, Mary, and Joseph. I know I struggle all the time to be the kind of parent I want to be. Did they struggle, too? It's hard enough being a parent to a regular kid. It must have been awesomely stressful to be Mom and Dad to God. Didn't Jesus ever give them any trouble? What would *they* do if Jesus wouldn't turn off the TV and go to bed? Didn't Mary and Joseph ever argue about whose turn it was to empty the dishwasher? Didn't she ever worry whether the family was getting enough time together?

I don't know the answers to these questions, but I do believe prayer and reflection are the best way to search for wisdom in dealing with these everyday family issues. I think Mary and Joseph offer parents a unique understanding of our stresses and hopes, and I am grateful for the strength and comfort I have found there.

*Pat Wingert Kelly, a Washington correspondent for* Newsweek magazine, *and her husband Brian have three children: Daniel, Laura, and Jack Ryan.*

# The Lesson of the M&M's

*Doreen C. Engel*

Motherhood brings great joys and great sorrows, both of which have the power to lead us closer to God. I want to focus here on the joys.

The joys of motherhood are too numerous to count. But though they may be countless, they can be categorized, and I would number the categories at four: creation, relation, action, and contemplation.

*Creation.* The joys of creation arise from giving birth and watching a child grow to maturity. I would choose the births of my two children, Danny and Gregory, as the two most amazing events I have experienced. In the passion according to St. John, Jesus uses the analogy of a woman in labor to try to prepare his apostles for how they soon will be feeling. Jesus speaks of a woman who knows her time has come and is sorrowful. But after she gives birth to her child, she forgets her pain because of her joy "of having brought a human being into the world" (John 16:21).

What I find amazing about this are the very last words. I would expect it to read "because she now has a baby." Upon reflection, however, I realized that my experience of giving birth really was one of rejoicing because a child had been born *into the world*. The joy was so enormous that it was more than just for my husband and me. It really was joy for the entire

116

world. I recall being absolutely astounded at the beauty of creation and thinking to myself: everyone who has ever lived has come into the world in almost just the same way. Amazing.

*Relation.* Once the child is created and born into the world, a mother has the wonderful experience of relating to the child. *Motherhood* in its most basic definition is the relationship between a woman and a child. It is a relationship of particular intimacy and longevity. It is continually used throughout the Bible as the example of God's love for us. We read in Isaiah 49:15, "Can a woman forget her nursing child, / or show no compassion for the child of her womb? / Even these may forget, / yet I will not forget you."

My grandmother passed away at the age of 101. During our last visit, we spoke, as we often did, about our children. My grandmother had four children. The oldest two, my father and my Uncle Lou, were born twenty months apart, just like my two boys. So of course my boys reminded my grandmother of her two oldest sons. During that last visit, she told me about a typical day in her life while caring for my father and my uncle when they were five-and-a-half and four, the same age as my boys. What a memory! She was recalling events of more than seventy years ago with great precision and clarity: the clothes her sons wore, the foods they liked, their companions, their complaints. It seemed she had forgotten very little, and I can easily believe that if I reach that age I, too, will remember my children with that same depth of intimacy.

Just as I will never forget my children, my children are probably old enough now to never forget me. Now that they have known me emotionally, mentally, and physically as their mother, they will never be able to have another woman as their mother. I am the only human being, of the billions of people in the world, who can be their mother. This is a very humbling thought, which to me emphasizes in a very concrete way my uniqueness in God's eyes.

At the same time, motherhood has the ability to remind me that I am very much like all other mothers. I had this experience in a vivid way when Danny was about six months old. I was visiting a group home for the mentally ill where my husband worked, and I had Danny with me. A woman came up to me with a shoebox with a few pictures inside. The pictures were of the same small boy and always showed him in front of a birthday cake. She told me, "This is my son. I couldn't take care of him because I am a schizophrenic, so I placed him for adoption. Every year on his birthday, his mother sends me a picture of him." Then she walked away, sat down in a rocking chair, and began to rock with the shoebox on her lap. With this brief encounter, I felt that I had a great deal in common with both her and the woman who had mailed those pictures. All of us were trying to do the right thing for our little boys, as best we could.

*Action.* The relationship of motherhood leads naturally to the third category of joys, action. Caring for children requires a great deal of action—enough action to cause total exhaustion sometimes. And many of the activities required are things that I don't particularly like to do.

What has amazed me is that, sometimes, activities I really dislike become quite effortless and enjoyable when they involve my children. During my first pregnancy, I had gestational diabetes. So when I found out that I was expecting the second time, I immediately went on a very strict diet. I found this to be relatively easy to do. My husband often commented on how amazed he was that I found this to be no burden. As soon as Greg arrived, however, I abandoned that diet and would find it quite horrible to return to it. I am reminded of Jesus' words: "Come to me, all you that are weary and are carrying heavy burdens, and I will give you rest....For my yoke is easy, and my burden is light" (Matt 11:28, 30). I believe that if only I were able to love enough, then other things that I find quite difficult to do would become as effortless as that diet.

*Contemplation.* At first glance, contemplation and motherhood may appear to be mutually exclusive. But the joys of contemplation involve finding God in the everyday occurrences of family life.

While being a mother of small children does not leave much time for contemplation, it makes up for it by providing glorious inspiration. Psalm 131:2 reads: "But I have calmed and quieted my soul, / like a weaned child with its mother." What an astute observer this author was. There is indeed a very specific way that a young child sits on his mother's lap. The child is not hungry, not tired, not sorrowful, not playful. He is there because he is a child, and he wants to be with his mother. It is a great joy to me when my children sit with me this way. It has inspired me on many occasions, when I am too tired to pray in any other way, to picture myself with God simply because I am God's creature and he is my God.

A friend of mine is honestly described as a hard-nosed businessman. He has one son who is the same age as me. I remember complaining to him about how tired I was because I had been up at night with my children. He said: "Oh, my wife used to complain about the same thing. In fact, I often got up with Tom myself. I remember we had a little rocking chair by the window. I would put up the shade, settle Tom on my lap, and sit there looking out at the stars. And you know, as I sat there, I just knew that there was indeed a kind and loving God."

All in all, recounting the joys of motherhood reminds me of an incident that happened at our home recently. My small children received an M&M dispenser in the mail. After dutifully allowing them just so much candy, I placed it on top of the refrigerator, only to promptly open the refrigerator door. The dispenser came crashing down, spilling almost all the candy over the kitchen floor. Some of the candy was broken in the fall. My children were horrified. They started to cry and said, "Now we will have to throw the candy all away." Well, truthfully, the kitchen floor had just been washed that day, and I just couldn't bring myself to throw away all that beautiful candy. But I couldn't quite bring myself to put candy that had been on the floor back into the dispenser. So we did the only sensible thing: we ate it all. My husband was relaxing in the living room, and the boys and I took turns shuttling in handfuls of M&M's to him.

Like our fallen candy machine, motherhood offers more than enough joy and pleasure for all. It isn't all perfect, of course, but still very lovely. But you can't save any of it. At each opportunity, you take what you can, as much as you want, but that's it.

For me, the joys of caring for an infant now are gone. They went by very quickly and live only in my memory. Soon the joys of caring for young children will be replaced by those of having teenagers. (I refuse to believe that there are no such joys associated with teenagers.)

Dorothy Day, the founder of the Catholic Worker movement in America, attributed her first realization of God in her life as developing from the love she had for her daughter. Thus began a spiritual journey that many believe has warranted canonization. I do not find it surprising that Dorothy Day found the inspiration for sainthood in the love she had for her child. Rather, I find it surprising that I am not closer to God, considering the beautiful gift he has given me in the form of my two sons.

*Doreen C. Engel is director of the Benilde program at St. John's College High School in Washington, D.C., a program that gives students with special needs the opportunity to study a college preparatory curriculum. She and her husband Anthony are the parents of Daniel and Gregory.*

# Finding a Compass in Good Times and in Bad

*Judy O'Hara*

I have been given much by the Lord, most of it wonderful. I've been married since 1969 to my best friend, Bartley, with three great kids: Lizzy, Bartholomew, and Mary Ryan. But the Lord works in mysterious ways, and sometimes his gift has been heavy. Our son, Bart, took his life at the age of nineteen.

I have seen motherhood from both sides of the heart: the joy and wonder of gifts almost beyond measure, and then the terrible paralyzing sorrow when one of the treasured gifts is gone. The phone call every parent dreads came when Bart, a strapping blonde athlete, was away his first year at college. He died by carbon-monoxide poisoning. And even though he left us a loving note, we still don't have a lot of insight into exactly what made him feel such enormous pain that he would commit suicide.

That's how the fabric of my motherhood experience has been woven, and it is an important part of who I am. In spite of that—or more accurately, precisely because of that—I remain unshakably optimistic and filled with gratitude for the privilege of being a mother. It really is a privilege and, to me at least, something that remains an ongoing mystery and a constant source of awe.

When I talk about motherhood, I mean not just mothers through the miracle of birth but all the people who take on the role of mother in our society, all those who cast their mantle of caregiving around our children. What you have in motherhood is a wonderful mix of dreams and reality, hopes and fears, successes and setbacks, all held together by the connective tissue of unconditional love—and a strong measure of faith.

Unfortunately, they don't hand you any comprehensive set of rules as you embark on the motherhood adventure, no checklist to make sure you are coloring inside the lines. To be sure, there are plenty of road maps; parent-advice books fill whole aisles in the bookstores. The problem isn't finding a map. It's finding the compass, the magic magnetic arrow that points you unerringly in the right direction. The compass is essential to the journey.

Our own mothers prove to be a compass of sorts. My mother was gifted with a wonderful sense of humor and great wisdom that gave her the enviable ability to keep things pretty much in perspective. Her advice frequently came wrapped in sufficient humor to make it both palatable and memorable, but, of course, it was not always followed. For example, "Marry an orphan," she used to say; it eliminates in-law problems. Talk about falling on deaf ears. I married the oldest of eight with relatives as far as the eye could see.

My mother-in-law, one of the most welcoming people I ever knew, gathered me into her family as if I were one of her own. A widow at the age of forty-five with eight children trailing behind, she was a never-ending source of inspiration.

But motherhood remains a mystery to me. Just when you think you are getting the hang of it, suddenly the sands shift, and you find yourself searching for a new foothold. It's almost as if the goal of competence—like the fruit to Tantalus—is always just out of reach.

The early challenges—sleeping through the night and tantrum management—too soon give way to the nursery school and kindergarten years, when your refrigerator becomes an art gallery and life's discoveries expand beyond fingers and toes to the world outside.

Speaking of discovery, when our Bart was in kindergarten, he was studying phonics in class one day by cutting out pictures and pasting them next to matching words. Halfway into this exercise, up went his hand to tell the teacher he didn't know what one of the pictures was. Turns out it was a picture of an iron. Obviously, I am not a compulsive housekeeper.

The middle years I like to think of as the time when the children are old enough to dress themselves, but still too young to get arrested. These years are crammed with action: scouts, sports, music lessons, braces, schoolwork, sleepovers, car pools, loose teeth, science projects, and that's just the short list. The trick is to maintain the balancing act and to make sure the parent hours are dispensed in defensible portions.

Enter that ear-piercing whine: "But Mm-o-o-o-mmm, you're not being fair." (Incidentally, when *Mom* becomes a four- or five-syllable word, you know you're in for rough seas.) Anyway, when you're accused of not being fair, it does spark the hidden doubts: Are they right? Am I being unfair? Where is the compass when I need it?

The subject of being fair reminds me of an essay by our friend Phyllis Theroux, in which she compares raising three children to growing a gardenia, a cactus, and a tub of impatiens." Each needs differing amounts of water, sunlight, and pruning," she writes. "Will one child learn about delayed gratification? Will another child ever feel confident? Will a third understand that honesty's reward is peace of mind?"* Just when one child needs a firm hand, another needs the gentle breeze of forgiveness. As a mother, I have come to appreciate that equal and fair are two entirely different things.

The high school years, so alive with growth and transformation, stretch a parent's mind and heart in every conceivable way. Driving lessons, prom parties, the "beach week" debate, SATs, college applications, expanding horizons, and growing confidence. I remember coming home one afternoon to a brilliantly smiling Lizzy, who had endured five years of orthodontia. Seeing her obediently aligned teeth without their customary wire, I said, "Wow, I thought the orthodontist never would take your braces off." "He didn't," replied a fully empowered Lizzy. "I did, with a Swiss army knife and the tweezers." While I am certain the parent books would have prescribed meaningful dialogue about patience or something else at this point, my gut reaction was: *Yes! Way to go, Lizzy!* I'll score that one for the compass.

_____

*Phyllis Theroux, *Night Lights* (New York: Penguin Books, 1987) pp. 30 and 50.

The college adventure in applied-life experiences takes on a sort of surrealistic hue. We know there's a lot going on, but it's all happening outside of our jurisdiction. The casual parental query—"So, what did you do this weekend?"—is fielded deftly by the universal "Not much." This from a child on a campus awash with activity and adventure. The conversational ball never gets out of the infield.

But there also are brilliant moments of validation we treasure. I am thinking of one Mother's Day present from our Mary Ryan. Weeks earlier I had offered some unsolicited—and I am fairly certain unwanted—advice about something. I think the issue was parking tickets, but that really is of no importance.

"Hi Mom," chirped Mary Ryan. "I'm calling with your Mother's Day present."

"Oh," I said, "and what would that be?"

"Mom, I should have listened to you. You were right."

Is there a better present than that? Instant validation. It certainly compares favorably with the white mouse the kids gave me for Mother's Day many years earlier.

And then suddenly they are launched, bathed in the protective warmth of our love that surrounds them like sunshine and armed with whatever wisdom we have scattered through their heads and hearts. They are off to careers and lives with mysteries of their own. Then we watch and pray, with an occasional tablespoon of advice thrown in every now and again.

Motherhood and fatherhood require lots of change. The trouble with change is that most often it involves letting go. Doing so with grace and faith is the ultimate challenge.

We have chosen not to spend an unhealthy measure of time and emotional energy trying to understand why Bart ended his young life. The answer to that question lies so deeply within Bart's perception of himself and the world around him that it simply isn't ours to know. Life doesn't allow us to stay in place. So we have chosen to move forward, rather than backward.

A parent's life is forever changed by the loss of a child, but we resolved not to let our lives be defined by that loss. Mary Ryan best describes our life without Bart. She says it's like having a hole in your living-room floor. You become very good at walking around it, but it never goes away. And the worst thing you can do is put a rug over it.

The path that all parents travel is filled with twists and turns. Being married to your best friend, particularly when the going gets really rough, is a gift beyond measure. So is the community of which we are blessed to be a part. The prayers and support that have been showered on our family are simply breathtaking.

After all is said and done then, the compass remains the key. The compass of our faith and love, surrounded by a community of support and strength, is the magic magnetic arrow that points us true north.

*Judy O'Hara, an attorney in private practice, and her husband Bartley, also an attorney, are the parents of Lizzy, Mary Ryan, and Bartholomew, who died on his nineteenth birthday in February 1993.*

# Grace and Fear

## *Elayne Bennett*

I was going to call this piece "I Have a Dream," but my husband, Bill, told me it's been copyrighted. When you anthologize as many things as Bill does, you take copyright seriously, let me tell you.

And I'm not going to speak about virtues—except that of being a mother, which should be the ultimate virtue. Notice I said *should be.* There are a lot of places—from the meanest streets to the highest boardroom—where there is precious little virtue in being a mother.

Instead my topic is "The Grace and Fears of a Mother." Why is it, mothers, that the greatest grace comes to us on the heels of the greatest fear or loss?

A friend recently asked me what my biggest fright was as a mother. Let me take you there briefly before I get to the grace. The scene was Georgetown University Hospital. I had just given birth to our first son, John Robert Glover Bennett, three weeks too soon. The baby was jaundiced; he was so small he fit completely into Bill's hand, with the feet barely dangling over.

I entered motherhood intensely. I just locked onto this child, an instant bond born at least partly out of fear for him. When they tested the bilirubin count by taking blood from the heel of his foot, I held him and cried.

John's early entrance wasn't my only surprise. The doctors had predicted a girl. Bill didn't know I knew this, but I'd quietly told my best friend that this was a girl and that we were calling the child "Mary." When Bill called my friend with the good news, he told her: "It has ten toes, and ten fingers, and a penis."

"Well, is it a boy or a girl?" asked my confused friend. "You know," Bill told me later, "I don't think your friend is very smart." That's when I confessed that I had withheld the doctor's prediction of a girl, knowing that Bill had wanted a boy, but also knowing he would instantly love any child we had.

John had to overcome more than jaundice and coming out early to see us. He had serious asthma as a baby. I must have covered five thousand miles in the rocking chair. John didn't sleep through the night until he was two. He would wheeze and whistle, trying to gain breath. And I would sing him every song I knew. No wonder he didn't sleep!

Thank God, John grew out of asthma at age four. Thank God, I insisted that doctors not give him the Theophylin they wanted to give him, which research now has shown inhibits development. And thank God that I didn't take the morphine the doctors wanted to give me when I was going into labor, which can slow respiration in premature babies. These are the sorts of fears mothers endure. Mothers, beware. It isn't just the illegal drugs you have to watch.

John now is the fastest boy in the seventh grade. When we see him run, we feel God's pleasure. As a teenager, he loves lacrosse and basketball and plays with such great intensity that he is frankly, if not graceful, pure desire and grace, just as is his brother, Joe, though their graces are different.

Our dear son Joe also had early asthma. I vividly recall one night of breathing difficulties, when the doctor at 2 a.m. told me to hold the phone to Joe's mouth so he could hear the child's wheezing. We were ordered to take him immediately to Children's Hospital across town. That happened to be the same night Bill resigned as drug czar for President George H. W. Bush. Let me tell you, the minute you leave such a government post, the federal marshals assigned for security immediately disappear. There is no grace period. They just disappear. That night we could have used their help.

So there we were getting lost in a tough part of town late at night. Bill stopped the car and took off to chase down a bus for directions to Children's Hospital. He finally prevailed on a street fellow for directions. All the while, I was praying, "God help us if he should be recognized by a drug dealer!"

Thank God, Joe was free of asthma before he was three years old. Thank God, he is a gifted, sensitive, tall nine-year-old boy who wrote this for me on Valentine's Day: "Love is very, very melting and you feel very good. But there's one very bad part about it. You have to spend a lot of money on the jewelry. Sometimes you play games with each other, like basketball. Most of the times you have fun. Love is the most special gift that you can give someone."

I wasn't a mother until I was thirty-four. I wasn't married until I was thirty-two. For many years, I would hold my friends' children longer than they held them themselves.

There were times it was very hard to hand them back. There were many, many nights when I was a very sad young woman, a graduate student in Chapel Hill, North Carolina, getting older, but not wiser.

Then a friend, who we've since decided was an angel, set me up with a blind date in Raleigh. This blind date asked me over the phone, "Do you have a car?" "Great," I thought. "Another slacker. Doesn't have a car. The only good thing about this deal is that I can drop him off early and get out of there fast."

Well, I went to meet him at the National Humanities Center, expecting a bearded, bespectacled academic, the skinny type, maybe with a knapsack. I bumped into this curly-haired, strong young guy in the foyer and I told him, "I'm looking for Bill Bennett." And what did this fellow say? "What took you so long? You're late!" I've been late ever since.

If you believe in love at first sight, this was pretty close to it. We were married about a year later in the same place I first met him, and I'll never forget the light hitting his curly hair just the same way it had the year before. I think I will always see the light on my husband's forehead, even when the curly hair is gone.

He was thirty-nine that day. I like to think I made him a little younger. He certainly has made me happy. If you want to be a good mother, there is no substitute for a good husband. Bill helps John with math each night. He goes to the boys' CYO basketball games. There is no political banquet that will take him from watching those boys run and leap. I'm a late bloomer. There is no one I would rather have bloomed with, late or not, than my William J. Bennett, father of Joe and John.

Both Bill and I were blessed with incredible mothers. My role model is my mother, Dorothy Glover, known as "Dotty." To put it simply, she was and is a ball of fire. I would not compare her to that traditional female image of the moon. She was the sun, plain and simple, and the whole family revolved around her, were warmed by her, and were kept in place by her. My mother was a nurse and taught nursing. In fact, she rolled up her sleeves and helped John come into the world when the nurses on duty got swamped by a birthing boom at the hospital that night.

She liked me to read to her. I remember reading her *The Yearling*. I recall her rushing to school in her nurse's uniform to direct the Brownie Scout Troup in making stuffed animals. My mom was from the Midwest, a presence of tolerance and practicality. She was not a "steel magnolia"—more like a "steel sunflower": not sweet, but a giver of shade even as she warmed you. And those sunflower seeds were healthy.

I'll never forget her fashioning a blue silk headpiece for me when I played the Virgin Mary in the third-grade Christmas play, with my one great line, "Oh, Joseph, I'm so weary!" Poor Joseph. He looked terrible in a bathrobe, and the second graders said so. But the lovely costume my mother made was my first clear recognition that my mother was really smart and that she used her brains for me. Mothers, is there a better thing to use our brains for than our children?

Finally, this leads me back to grace. I'm a convert to the Catholic faith, and Mary is my great joy in the Catholic Church. Mary is not emphasized in Protestantism. Her presence is, frankly, muted. But look at what we say here? "Hail, Mary, full of grace." The word *grace*. There is no fear I won't encounter for a chance at that grace. It is part of Mary, the mother of God. It is part of mothers.

Are we mothers losing grace in this world of the quick retort, the sarcastic comment, pervasive on television and in the movies, that you hear day to day as you go about your work? We live in a world where everything is supposed to be ironic and fast paced. I have seen a toughness develop in women; is it because we often must put our instinctive nurturing aside to compete in the daily grind?

Well, *I* have a dream: that mothers in this society are proud once again of grace, and gracefulness, and graciousness. We've earned it. And no paycheck or status can equal it.

It is my true wish on Mother's Day that every child is mothered, whether by his or her birth mother or by a mother who comes into that child's life by the grace of God.

My dream is that mothers are respected for the most important job they or anyone will ever have, and that employers will respect motherhood and give women the flexibility they need in the workplace to tend to their children's doctors, teachers, schools, and playtime.

I have a dream that we never lose the notion of a mother's irreplaceable instinct or a mother's touch.

I have a hope that we mothers return to creating memories in our own backyard, rather than relying on disinterested, pre-packaged birthday zones.

Every day I work and pray that young girls will not become mothers until they are mature adults so that they can know the joy of being young and can develop the self-worth so necessary to good motherhood.

My greatest wish is this: that when my boys are men, they will choose as wives women who are strong as the sun, happy as a sunflower, and as loving and full of grace as Mary.

*Elayne Bennett is founder of the Best Friends Program, a character-building curriculum for adolescent girls that has been recognized as one of the nation's most effective programs in preventing teen pregnancy. She is married to William Bennett, former White House advisor on drug policy and former education secretary. He is also editor of the* Book of Virtues *series. Their children are John and Joseph.*

# Outside Our Comfort Zone

*Susanne Risher Kersey*

My mother, Bernice Risher, was born and raised in segregated Alabama with, as she always put it, two strikes against her: both black and Catholic. She told stories of her first-hand experiences with racism. One story in particular I remember was how the Ku Klux Klan had surrounded the Catholic elementary school she attended and the children could not leave until late that night. As you know, the Klan is anti-Catholic, as well as anti-Jewish and anti-black. The nuns led a prayer vigil. Finally the Klansmen left, and my mother and the other children were able to go home.

When she finally moved to Washington, D.C., in 1943, the situation was not much better. The schools and churches were segregated. To this day, my mother still has a hard time sitting in the front of a church; when she arrived here, the blacks were seated in the back and whites in the front. All of these experiences had a profound effect on her. Because my mother was restricted from interacting with different people as a child, she actively sought out and developed friendships with people from different backgrounds and cultures as an adult.

It's incredible to think of all the sacrifices my mother made in bringing me up. She was a young divorced parent. We lived in Northeast D.C. in a one-bedroom apartment midway between Howard University and Catholic University. Anyone who knows my mother knows that she has a very outgoing and gregarious personality that attracts people. When I was a child, we lived in a very small apartment, but we always had someone sleeping on our couch. There were people from all walks of life, with all sorts of personal crises, and from all over the world. It was our own United Nations. Some came for a couple of days to sort things out. Others stayed while they completed their higher education.

They repaid my mom in many ways. A Jewish woman taught me to swim. A Puerto Rican woman who came for a weekend stayed quite a while and taught me to make a mean potato salad. Once we had a young woman from Pakistan live with us for six months while she attended Howard University Medical School. As a result of these many friendships, I toured Europe with a French woman and her daughter and spent three months traveling the Riviera.

You have to understand—that was really a big deal for me. At the time, not too many ten-year-olds in my neighborhood could venture anywhere outside the immediate metropolitan area. But here I was, spending a summer in Europe. Although my mother could not afford to go with me, she was committed to broadening my horizons and letting me experience life outside of our Northeast D.C. neighborhood. When I got older and started earning money, I took every opportunity to travel: Africa, the Caribbean, whenever I could afford to go.

My mother also exposed me to different cultures and people through the arts and music. When I was young, there weren't the organized weekend activities that I have suc-cumbed to with our two daughters. My mother would take me to a museum or a concert. We would be at Lisner Auditorium watching the dancers of Bali, or Crampton Auditorium watching the Kenyan dancers, or even at the Shoreham Hotel watching Jose Greco and the Flamenco dancers at the dinner show. "Rish," as she was known, could not afford to put me on a jet plane, but she was determined that I would see the world that was available in my own backyard.

It's only now, as a parent myself, I can truly appreciate the foundation my mother created. She is responsible for my becoming the person I am today. I, too, think of myself as a "people person," and I am trying to raise my daughters in the same tradition.

The challenges for me—for all of us as parents today—are different but no less difficult. Our nation grows more diverse, but our people are still polarized.

Among the few luxuries we have as a family are the occasional social times with family or friends on weekends. In all the craziness of the world, one of the comforts in life is being with people you feel close to because you share a com-mon bond. You grew up together, or you are neighbors, or your kids go to school and church and camp together. Let's face it. We all have the tendency to want to be with our own kind. It's a comfortable setting. Why venture out?

Why? Because we have to! All of us would like our short time on earth to be in a comfortable, nonthreatening environment with people who are just like us. But that ideal stunts both our social and spiritual growth. The real world outside is multicultural, multireligious, and multiracial, and getting more so every day—this great country of ours in particular and this city specifically. It is our job as parents to help our children prepare for a future of merging and interacting within this melting pot. We do this by laying the groundwork now. The way we prevent a future of skinheads, Ku Klux Klan members, or Aryan Nation groups is to expose our children to people who are different, whether in looks, culture, nationality, color, class, or religion. In doing this, our children not only gain a better understanding of tolerance and acceptance, but they learn true appreciation. And they make new friends.

I'm sure all of us would like to strive for a color-blind society. It won't be possible until we can appreciate and embrace our differences. Only then can we accept that, in God's eyes and, in turn, our eyes, we have immense similarities despite our differences. We are more alike than different. Our differences allow us to offer unique opportunities to others. We have to take small steps in any way we can to help our children become good, spiritual, loving adults.

When our girls were younger, they attended a synagogue preschool in our neighborhood. It was an enlightening experience for them, as well as for my husband Franklin and me. To see them with yarmulkes on their heads and have them teach us the Jewish prayer for Shabbat was a treat. I remember in the month of February, Alexis was learning about the Jewish holiday of Purim with Haman and Queen Esther. She also was learning about Abe Lincoln. Sometimes the lessons became a little confused. She came home one day and announced that she knew everything about Abe Lincoln. What do you know? I asked. Well, he was president of the United States, he was killed, but before he died, he saved all the Jews.

My daughter Ashley absolutely hated taking ballet and had no interest in tap or modern dance. She came home this past year and announced she absolutely had to take Irish dancing. Well, Franklin and I didn't think there was much future for our African American daughter as an Irish step dancer. But then again, who knows? She's taking it now and loves it. This year, Franklin and I watched her in the St. Patrick's Day Parade. And maybe ten years from now, the group Riverdance will be performing at Wolf Trap amphitheater, and as the camera pans across the stage, there will be the "O'Kersey" family's brown-faced, black-haired daughter skipping across the stage. A true "black Irish."

Just small steps are needed to make a difference in the world. Sometimes the efforts will be uncomfortable and challenging, but we have a responsibility to do it. Maybe we can expose our children to diversity through the arts, or enlighten them with books that explore different cultures, or take them to a historical landmark such as the Frederick Douglass House right here in D.C. Maybe we engage them in a social-action project, or maybe we just send them to a summer camp that is more diverse with fewer of the friends they see on a regular basis.

But most importantly, we need to talk to our children. One of parents' biggest challenges is knowing when to approach children to discuss certain topics, whether it be drugs, alcohol abuse, human sexuality, or any other complicated subject. Never in my wildest dreams did I think that I would have to broach the issues of bigotry and prejudice with my children at the young ages of four and seven, but it happened. We were on an annual vacation trip in the South when my children heard the "*n* word" for the first time. It was directed at us. Franklin and I had to compose ourselves and suppress our anger long enough to sit in a car and explain racial prejudice to our young and innocent daughters. As horrible and personally degrading as that experience was, we seized the opportunity to explain the burdens of color and the realities of prejudice.

That incident has gone a long way in helping us have open and candid discussions with our children about gender bias, discrimination against individuals with disabilities, and yes, even homosexuality. Let's face it, we are not with our children 100 percent of the time, and our children develop opinions and talk to each other about these issues. It's critical that parents recognize we are the primary opinion makers. We know that children do not invent bigotry and prejudice. Their parents do.

We live in a time and world of turmoil. We live in a city with crime. Our children watch the news on television and are often confronted with troubling and disturbing images. Most of the time, it is very unbalanced. Unfortunately, the media does not offer enough positive images to offset the negative portrayals. As mothers, we have the responsibility to overcome the stereotypes and negative images by enlightening our children that people of all colors are both good and bad and by instilling in them that people are to be judged by the content of their characters and not by their color or gender.

We mothers must aggressively pursue integrating our children with the world outside. My mother took the challenge with me. I intend to follow her footsteps. I hope that you will join me.

*Susanne Risher Kersey is an editor for public television's NewsHour with Jim Lehrer. She and her husband Franklin, an attorney, are the parents of Alexis and Ashley. Susanne Risher Kersey's mother, Bernice Risher, died January 17, 2001.*

# Stairway to Heaven

*Barbara Rosewicz*

A few years ago, the first thing I probably would have told you about myself is that I'm a journalist. Nowadays I'm much more likely to describe myself first and foremost as the mother of three boys. My identity is so bound up with my children than even standing here alone at church feels unnatural; I'm so used to having one of my boys holding my hand, tugging on my skirt, or trying on my jewelry during Mass.

I need to say I stand here humbly. I wish we could have found a real Supermom to illuminate us with answers to some of the burning questions of motherhood today. Well, I readily confess I'm not that Supermom. Like many, I'm groping for that right balance between work and children. I even have to wonder about my maternal values when perhaps the best part of today's Mother's Day gift was that my husband, Jerry Seib, took all three children out shopping yesterday, and I had three hours alone. Home alone. A rare treat.

No, I don't have answers for modern mothers. I don't know why finding and keeping good childcare is so difficult. I'm always wondering: why do my sons have more active social lives than I do? I was stumped by my son Jake, who at five asked, "Is there a stop to space?" And, yes, I have given some thought to this ethical dilemma, but I can't tell you how many Beanie Babies are indeed too many.

I can share, though, a personal revelation about motherhood that came as a surprise. It's the spiritual side of motherhood. It isn't something you can pick up from Penelope Leach or T. Berry Brazelton or any of those bibles for new mothers.

It's even different from that heavy-duty first dose of spiritual responsibility you get at your child's baptism. Think back to when your child was baptized. You take an oath to fight off Satan himself, and now you're not only responsible for your own sorry soul but also for the everlasting soul of another human being, too. It's an awesome vow.

But those promises were of what I was going to give the child, do for my child. What I didn't count on was what motherhood was going to give *me* in terms of strengthening my own relationship with God.

It's appropriate that I share with you this revelation, even though, frankly, I thought I'd never talk about this private an experience to anyone. It happened one Sunday right here at this Mass. I like to think of it as a moment of grace. Father Percival D'Silva had gathered all the children around the altar for the consecration. I looked out and could see my oldest son sidling up to his friends. I watched as other parents' heads bobbed out into the aisle to check on whether their little ones were behaving in front of the altar. I felt a strong kinship at that moment with all the parents in the congregation. We were all wrapped up in the same struggles, from the everyday hassles like how to handle carpools and sick days, to the overarching concerns like how to raise ethical kids with values beyond money and with religious roots to last them a lifetime.

And I had a stunning realization. I could almost picture a stairway unfolding from above, before my eyes. The thought struck me: Hey, Barbara, *this* is how you get to heaven. If you don't botch this up, this is the way God has laid out for you to achieve salvation.

Suddenly I realized that all of my maternal struggles— to be the best mom in the world, to perform all the unglamorous chores of parenting with super efficiency, to give my kids a good religious grounding, and somehow to take time to smell the roses—weren't just some personal challenge that tested my mettle. This was bigger. This was a mission from God. This was a way I could perfect myself. Hey, this could be my ticket to heaven.

I think that was the first time I truly accepted motherhood as my vocation. Like Isaiah being called by God in the song by Dan Schutte that we often sing: "Here I am Lord. Is it I, Lord? I have heard you calling in the night...." Well, that was the day I heard.

All of this doesn't mean that I think moms need to chuck their professional careers into the dumpster and stay home fulltime with their kids to get to heaven. But it made a difference in my life when I realized that my career, despite its many rewards, had never offered me a way to heaven.

Motherhood also blessed me with another heavenly insight. I can now better understand God's love for me, for all of us, on a different level. A mother's love is like God's love. It is an unconditional love. It reminds me of conversations you have with your child when he or she has just told you, "I don't love you anymore," and "I want a new mom (or dad.)" Once you get a grip on yourself, you tell the child that you love him no matter what. You don't always love what he says; you don't always love what he does. But you love him no matter what. That's like God's love for us. God doesn't love us because we're lovable, thank God. Like a mother, he loves us just because we're his children. That's very reassuring.

I can better understand now how God still loves me even when I don't quite hold up my end of the relationship. This reminds me of my own mother, Bernice Rosewicz, who lives in Kansas City. She's been writing me a letter every week since 1981 when I moved away from Kansas (except when I'm there for a visit). I write her on holidays and birthdays, sending new pictures of the grandkids; I phone now and then; but for a newspaper reporter, I'm not nearly as faithful a correspondent as she is. My mother gives willingly, even though I don't repay her in equal measure. That's like God's love for us.

And like a mother, God is forgiving of us. My own mother forgave me when, as a kid, I left a permanent brand in the shape of a hot steam iron on the new wall-to-wall carpet in the new house my father had just built for our family. Well, I remembered this not too long ago when my boys gleefully threw plastic darts at a target they'd attached to the living-room fireplace, and left pockmarks all over the wooden mantel. God will forgive us, too, even when our transgressions are far greater than pockmarks in the woodwork.

Lastly, being a mother has made me lean on God even more, often through intercessions to the Blessed Virgin. There's a ritual I follow every night in my house. It's something my own mother did. I don't even know whether my boys know about this. Every night before I go to bed, I tiptoe into each boy's room and make the sign of the cross in the dark over their heads. It's my way of telling God I am trusting him to care for my children in all those times and places I can't.

*Barbara Rosewicz, former reporter for* the Wall Street Journal *recently returned to the workplace, after some time home with her children, to become deputy managing editor of* Stateline.org, *an online news publication that reports on state governments. She and her journalist husband Gerald Seib have three sons: Joseph, Jacob, and Lucas.*

# Adoption Is Like a Marriage

*Trish Warner*

I associate becoming a mother with airplanes, airports, courtrooms, a mountain of paperwork, years of yearning, and the sudden shock that the dream had become reality. I've been blessed with two children. They are miracles in my life. They came to me through adoption.

I met my older daughter, Cathleen, when she was five days old. I first studied her perfection on the tray table of a jet airplane. We met Maria when she was a few months short of three years old. She was waiting in an airport seven thousand miles from here in Paraguay. Her guardian told us she brought her to the airport because she had been pointing at airplanes for weeks asking for us. Maria met her sister, grandparents, aunts, uncles, and cousins in other airports. "Fly the Friendly Skies" has real meaning for our family.

In the years since the first thrilling phone call about Cathleen—Father's Day 1982—we've had plenty of time to settle in, find out about each other, and come to grips with both the past and the future. What has all this meant to us? How has adoption affected our lives? How has it affected my viewpoint?

I recommend adoption to anyone who loves suspense, mystery, and surprise. It amuses me to think back to when I insisted on surprises on birthdays. Now I have them every day. Most people assume that the surprises for families like us have to do with surprising differences. I enjoy our differences. But I've been more surprised by the similarities. I see my mother's traits in Cathleen, a grandmother's characteristics in Maria. I learned when Maria joined us that children really are the same all over the world, even if cultural norms differ. I've taken the meaning of global village into my heart because I love her so much.

Our everyday life is ordinary. We cope with decisions about television, schoolwork, how many times a week to have pizza, appropriate friends, what kind of pizza to eat, suitable clothes, and what videos to rent while we eat pizza. We celebrate a lot. Because Maria is Hispanic and from South America, our family culture has some added spice. On St. Patrick's Day, we talk about the Irish in Paraguay. We remember the statue of a historian, Juan O'Leary, in Asuncion. We've discovered that, due to Jesuit influence, the harp is the national instrument of Paraguay and that, like the Irish, Paraguayans make lace—and they also make beer. I've told Maria about visiting the Port of Kinsale in Ireland. The Spanish landed at that spot, and you can see their long black cloaks in the Kinsale museum.

Adoption has also meant coming to terms with our losses, accepting a shared fate, and coping with having only shadowy details of very important personal history. I don't know whether the future will offer a strong sense of identity for my children. If they decide to lift the veil on the past, I will be holding their hands.

Because of adoption, I feel a special empathy for women facing pregnancy as a crisis. They need respect, emotional and financial support, encouragement, uncritical counseling, and friends who will help them. Some will make an adoption plan, trusting God to secure the future of their children. They need help dealing with this decision long after it is made, long after the children have gone to other homes. If you know them, please reach out. Let them know adoptive families love and admire them. We see their image in the faces of the children.

Because of adoption, my definition of mother is broader than it once was. I think Mother's Day should recognize all the women who encourage and care for children.

A friend called me recently to tell me adoption is mentioned in the Bible. I listened carefully because my children have given me a renewed sense of faith. She said that when she brought her son home from South America, her father, a minister, took her aside. He told her we are all sons of God through adoption and showed her Paul's Epistle to the Romans (Rom 8:14, 15). I like that. We are all God's adopted children and heirs through Christ.

Someone else once mentioned to me that adoption is like a marriage. I like that, too. My bond with my children is intense, and this added a sense of being linked in a permanent spiritual union with them. I read the wedding vows I wrote in 1978 and realized that many of them apply to both my husband and my children. This week I looked at them again. It seems appropriate to read them on Mother's Day as a pledge to children everywhere from mothers everywhere:

"Your joys will be mine; your sadness will be ours to share. In fortune and misfortune, in health or illness, I will cherish you and will be near you with understanding, compassion, and warmth. You can depend on my love forever."

*Trish Warner, a senior analyst for Pal-Tech, Inc., a consulting group that supports federal programs, is married to John. Their children are Cathleen and Maria.*

# God Is Reading Us

*Mickey Edwards*

In keeping with Blessed Sacrament tradition, I would like to offer some family stories. My children, Jessica and Andy, have pleaded with me not to embarrass them. Only after I readily assured them they had nothing to worry about did it dawn on me that for a 16-year-old and a 13-year-old, *any* story I told about them would embarrass them, no matter how innocuous it might seem to me. The result is that my material is limited to past generations and collateral relatives. If at any time I slip and appear to be talking about some actual child of mine, keep in mind that it is the purest work of fiction not intended to resemble any living person.

To begin, come back with me to a kitchen in an old frame house in Zanesville, Ohio. The year is 1918, and it is Saturday morning. My Hungarian immigrant grandmother is doing her weekly baking. Her five children are scattered at chores and at play, and my grandfather is working overtime at the steel mill. Carefully my grandmother arranges a pile of fragrant warm donuts on a large platter in the middle of the table and walks out of the kitchen. My mother and her brothers and sisters and their friends creep quietly into the room, and in a few seconds the platter is empty. My grandmother returns to the now-empty kitchen, looks at the table, and exclaims in Hungarian, "I thought I put a whole plate of donuts here! What happened to the donuts?" Every Saturday, the same scene is repeated.

When my mother told me this story from her childhood, she said that for years she could not understand why her mother did not just call the kids into the kitchen when the donuts were ready and dole them out. But when she became a mother herself, Mom understood what her mother was doing. The children had a need—not just for a snack, but for an adventure, some harmless mischief, a chance to play a prank on their mother. My grandmother loved them with a love that recognized that need. How like God's love for us, a love that knows and meets our needs.

Let's return to my grandmother's kitchen ten years later. My mother's long, blond pigtails have been replaced by a short curly 1920s cut. She is drinking coffee with her mother and pouring out her heart. At the YMCA in Zanesville, there are new bowling lanes where the young people can go in the evening. But my grandfather strictly forbids this. He knows from his steelworker friends that bowling alleys are places where men smoke and drink and swear, and no daughter of his will ever be seen in such a place! My mother is unable to convince him that the YMCA is a good Christian organization where no alcohol or swearing is permitted, and that bowling is an opportunity for fellowship and socializing. She pleads with him to come with her just once to see for himself, but he adamantly refuses. She turns to her mother. After hearing the story, her mother says simply, "You go on ahead with your friends, Margit. Don't tell your father." My mother was amazed that her mother would even think of defying her husband's rule. But my grandmother saw her daughter's need, the need to spend time with other young people, the need of a young adult for independence. Like God, she loved with a love that met that need.

Now travel with me to Wilmington, Delaware, in 1982. My sister Gigi is relating how my five-year-old nephew has had a terrible time sleeping because of nightmares about monsters. He calls them "Distles," and he is sure that they will come through the window and get him as soon as he gets into bed. My sister tries all the usual remedies, from night-lights to rational explanations to reassurances to "Hail Mary's"—all with no success. Every night, Matt screams out in fear and cannot get back to sleep. Finally, in desperation, Gigi says, "Matthew, I know what will protect you. Tonight we are going to line up all your stuffed animals on the window sill, and they will scare the Distles away." He thinks this is a very good idea. He sleeps that night and every night after, and to the best of my knowledge, no one has seen a Distle in Wilmington, Delaware, since 1982. His need was for a solution that fit his nonrational, nonscientific preschooler's view of the world. And, like God's love for us, his mother responded with a love that knew his need.

God's love also resembles a mother's love in another way; God loves us selflessly with a love that sets us free. That selfless maternal quality is often praised in Hallmark cards and newspaper feature stories. But when I think about my own family, I am struck with how that trait shows itself in a mother's letting go of her children—a letting go that begins when the children are still quite small.

When I was four, I was the last of four daughters, not yet in school, and my mother was the center of my universe. She was my constant companion, and I trailed her all over the house as she went about her daily chores. Still recovering from a devastating year of breast-cancer surgery and radiation treatment, she would get so tired in the afternoon that she would try to take a nap and persuade me to nap with her. But the moment her eyes were closed, I would wake her up because, as I told her, "When you close your eyes, I'm all alone." We spent so much time together that my earliest memories of church are from attending daily Mass with my mother during Lent. At the very smell of beeswax candles, those memories come flooding back.

Mom knew how much I needed to be with other kids. And so she enrolled me in a nursery school at Hazel Hawkins Happy Hour House. (Mrs. Hawkins liked alliteration.) As we walked up on the porch of that little establishment, I turned and, in the full maturity of one who was at last—like her big sisters—going to school, I said, "Now, don't hold my hand."

It was many years later that I realized there was a little catch in Mom's throat when she repeated that story. Did she go back to the car and shed a few tears, as I did when I took a child who shall remain nameless to sleep-away camp for the first time? I do know that my mother became practiced at letting go—my oldest sister to the convent at the age of eighteen where, in those pre-Vatican II days, Mary could make no phone calls home and could have only one two-hour visit a month; my second sister, Gigi, to the barrios of Lima, Peru, as a lay Catholic volunteer; and my third sister, Marty, to Germany to study theology. Surely by the time I went to college, Mom had become accustomed to the ache of separation. This is the selfless love of motherhood: a mother loves her children into freedom.

Of course the real blessing of motherhood—the secret that all the mothers here know—is that no matter how much we give our children, they give back a thousand times more. Sometimes, they even give us profound spiritual insights.

One day we were driving—probably late for a doctor's appointment—and were stuck in rush-hour traffic when my five-year-old, who shall remain nameless, queried, "Mom, are we real, or are we just characters in someone else's story?" Sensing that the best answer to a question you cannot answer is another question, I asked, "If we are characters in someone else's story, who is reading the story?" "God," my child responded, without a moment's hesitation.

Thank you for letting me share some tales from our family's chapter in the story God is reading.

*Mickey Edwards is a graduate student at the Washington Theological Union. She is the mother of Jessica Seidman and Andrew Seidman.*

# My Favorite Career

*Patricia Gaughan Burke*

"Congratulations, you're pregnant." Those are the words you hope for. "Congratulations, it's a healthy baby." Those are the words you pray for. "Mama, I love you." Those are the words that prove God is in heaven.

I have been blessed with this scene four times over: my daughter Maggie (named for my mom, Margaret McGovern), my daughter Molly, my daughter Katie, and my son Liam Jr. When you're only having one boy, you darn well make him a namesake.

I am simply a mom—not a Supermom, not a soccer mom, not a working mom. And I simply enjoy the daylights out of it. I worried after my second daughter was born and I had clearly made the decision to forgo an outside professional career that my parents might be upset. My mom worked hard at mothering fulltime and encouraged her girls to do anything in life they wanted. My parents had paid handsomely to send me to a private high school and Georgetown University. My brothers and sisters were lawyers, teachers, writers, business people. I worried and asked them, "Are you disappointed that I'm not using the education you worked so hard to pay for? Are you upset that I'm squandering all the resources you gave me?"

As the youngest of seven, I rarely saw a look of surprise on my dad's face, but I did that day. "Tricia, honey," he said.

"You're doing the best thing you could with your education. You'll need every bit of knowledge ever given you and then some." Obviously he was a very wise man. I constantly hark back not only to Psychology 101 and Intro to Philosophy, but also to my courses in fine arts, anthropology, physics, statistics, literature, theology. Every day a new question arises, a new situation where my response counts and will have repercussions throughout the lives of four human beings. To paraphrase Psalm 25, "Show me the path where I should go. Point out the right road for me to walk. Lead me. Teach me."

I take very seriously the responsibility of turning out four happy, giving, respectful, and successful people. God entrusted my husband, Liam, and me with four of his wonders.

But I also take very seriously the fun of being a mom, the license to never have to grow up. Little did Peter Pan know that the key to being young forever wasn't Neverland, but having your own children.

Play with them. Run through a field with abandon and fall down—even in your best white shorts. Make snow angels before breakfast. Kick a home run in your third-grader's kick ball game. "Rejoice in [the] day and leap for joy" (Luke 6:23).

I'm quite qualified to be a mom, not only because I come from a long line of them but also because, being the youngest of seven, I was mothered to death. It made me resilient and well-rounded. My older brothers and sisters had interests across the spectrum, so in idolizing all of them, I made it my business to learn about their loves: sports, politics, ballet, current events, acting, social justice. At age ten, when I decided on a name for my first daughter, whenever she might come along, I knew that it was this educational experience that would serve me well as a parent. Like my parents, I had seen it all, only from the other end.

I dreamt of what kind of child my Maggie would be and, of course, what a cool mom I would be. I even spoke to her, confiding in her and planning all the things we'd do. "Before I formed you in the womb I knew you" (Jer 1:5).

I couldn't be anything but a mom. All mothers feel the presence of God in their lives. We know the guardian angel who stops our toddlers right at the top of the staircase or lets them land on soft dirt from the monkey bars. We see the likeness of God in our newborns before we see our own. Alone at 3 a.m. in the nursery, rocking our babies cheek-to-cheek and feeling their light angel breath on our skin, in that nocturnal near-light we are closer to heaven than anywhere else on earth. This distinctive, tangible feeling of God's presence and love must be his gift to mothers. If we carry, nurture, and protect his most precious creation, then I suppose what we call "the maternal instinct" is actually an awareness of the divine purpose of our task and an acknowledgement of the presence of God in our roles.

To be a mother is, simply, a gift, a pure gift from God. And as with all gifts, we need to be thankful. And so, as Paul says to the Philippians, I say to my family, I thank God every time I think of you and in every prayer I say.

*Patricia Gaughan Burke* is currently working toward a liberal studies master's degree at Georgetown University. She and her husband Liam have four children: Maggie, Molly, Katie, and Liam Jr.

# Joy and Guilt

*Martha Kendrick Kettmer*

My husband Harry and I always planned to have children, but we wanted to be married a few years before we started a family. When we decided we were ready, we thought that, bingo, it would happen. Well, it didn't. As months dragged into a few years, infertility testing started, years of fertility drugs began, and the monthly pain of hoping and disappointment continued. Knowing that parenthood was our objective, we started into the adoption process. I began a diary so that our first child would know that whether he or she was adopted was irrelevant.

You know, we live in a world that allows us to think that we control our destinies and that *we* make the choices and decisions. My whole life up to that point underscored this perception: we make education choices, career choices, and relationship choices, including whom we date and whom we marry.

I wanted to become a mother more than anything I have wanted in my life, but it was not something I could make happen, either biologically or through adoption. I can vividly remember telling God, "I give up," accepting the fact that he probably didn't want me to become pregnant but still begging for a baby anyway, and finally putting it in his hands.

Our whole painful infertility experience was genuinely one of the faith cornerstones in my life.

Then I became pregnant with Christine. I have never been simultaneously so happy, hopeful, and scared in my life. To carry life within you, to feel the kicks and discomforts of pregnancy, is such a miraculous gift from God. I've been pregnant six times. My three miscarriages were heartbreaking, but I have three healthy children and consider myself the luckiest person on earth. I know that I have been blessed with three genuine miracles. I regularly tell my children they each enjoy a guardian angel in heaven.

No child has been more wanted than Christine, and she consistently has brought us happiness from the moment of her birth. Stated most simply, she's the greatest kid, thoughtful and loving; she helps so much and does so many things in life right. Our second child and first son is Tommy, whose smile lights up my life; no child I've ever seen spontaneously beams as he does. His challenging inquisitiveness, his determination, and his generosity make us proud and happy on a daily basis. And our brown-eyed Brian, who carries my family name as a middle name, is such a total gift, with his intellectual curiosity and logic, his impishness, toughness, competitiveness, his capacity for hugs, and his ability to make me smile and laugh. Each of our children lends such a special dimension to our family life. Each of them challenges me and makes me a better mother, a better parent.

As my mother taught me, I hope I am conveying to each of my children that each is a precious blessing and gift from

God, with individual, unique, and different strengths, but that our love for each is total.

Second lesson, no matter how old you are, Mother Mary stands as a model for each one of us. When my family faced the trauma of my father's six-month losing battle with leukemia, my mother demonstrated unwavering faith, endurance, and strength. She told me of the comfort she derived in realizing that Mary, the mother of God, experienced great earthly pain and suffering through Jesus' death. If God did not spare his own mother, then how could she complain about her own suffering?

My own Brian keeps me humble and with an eye on Mary as a model. He'll tell me with regularity, "Mom, you're the second-best mother in the world."

Mothers today face different challenges than a generation ago, especially mothers who work outside the home. Creating and nurturing connectedness to our kids' lives is at the core of motherhood. I thank God every day for the invention of the telephone, which allows me to get timely reports on school day and play experiences. I confess that I save some of my children's phone-mail messages so I can play them back and laugh if I need a good chuckle during the day. Tommy sang me a song several years ago that I still can't bear to erase from my phone-mail. Today I frequently save special e-mail messages to cherish them again later. Our modern communication wonders of cell phone, e-mail, and instant messaging all support and strengthen our parent-child communications from the workplace. Talking about everyone's day in the evening is an essential ritual.

There's no such thing as being a working mother without guilt. I know that I and other professional mothers try as best as we can to focus on every minute we can be with our children and to make up for the times our physical presence may not be there. My children are with me in spirit all day long.

When I was preparing recently for a women-in-the-law speech, I asked my children whether they were glad I am a lawyer. Each said yes. Christine is proud of my professional accomplishments as a woman; Tommy said he was glad because, if he ever needed a lawyer, he'd have his own; and Brian loves the soda machine in our law firm (he considers it a great bonus in his life). Each in his or her way articulated clearly the trade-offs, but their bottom line was their satisfaction. For their understanding and forgiveness and their attempts to assuage my guilt for the times a client or work or volunteer commitment has had to come first, I thank my children.

I tell my kids every day how much I love them and how lucky I feel. I try to reaffirm it each night at prayers with a goodnight kiss. I hope they know that my emotional support and love is with them each minute of every day and will be there every moment of their lives, just as I have felt my mother's with me every moment of my life.

My mother is in her eighties. Her four geographically dispersed daughters took her to Bermuda for a long golf weekend a few years back. She was especially grateful, I think, to her four sons-in-law for their domestic contributions to that first get-away weekend (now an annual ritual).

We had lots of fun, lots of shopping, and lots of laughs. But most of all, as daughters, we were struck once again by how much we owe our mother, who has demonstrated unwavering love, taught us Christian values, and given each of us so much of herself in so many countless ways. She's also a terrific role model as a grandmother; the way she has invested the time to create a special relationship with each of her twelve grandchildren reflects an ongoing commitment to the gift of life.

I may be doing it a little differently—with a lifestyle reflecting a bit more craziness—but my own mother always stands out as the kind of mother I want to be.

*Martha Kendrick Kettmer is a partner in the Washington, D.C., law firm of Patton Boggs LLP, specializing in health law and policy issues. She and her husband Harry are the parents of Christine, Tommy, and Brian.*

# Of Ladybugs and Grandma's Roses

*Martha Donnelly Paci*

Just as John Kennedy identified himself as the man who accompanied Jackie Kennedy to Paris, I am the little girl who accompanied Susie the dog to Sister Alice Teresa's first-grade class at Blessed Sacrament School during the 1960s. I hit my stride at the age of seven.

As both a biological and adoptive mother, I have diverse thoughts on how to approach the topic of motherhood. So I turn to my vocation as a landscape architect to provide metaphors to ruminations of motherhood—past, present, and future.

The seed grows, slowly, falteringly, and then robustly. The seed grows. And if it survives, the garden is readied for its placement. Our daughter, Jodi, was born after an emergency C-section. A dear friend and mother of four dropped onto my bed the day after surgery and said, "Isn't labor pain the best-kept secret in the world?" Years later, on a silent autumnal morning, Jimmy became my son at the age of four-and-a-half months. I will tell you that the pain of waiting, and not knowing if or when, was far greater than labor.

These are the beginnings of motherhood. And so my sprouts were planted in the garden of mankind. Just as soil,

165

air, and light feed the tree, so stories nourish the soul and instruct the character, and oral history begins.

Jodi, do you remember the day after Jimmy arrived? You were five years old and so thrilled to have a little brother that you selected your favorite stickers and plastered them all over him. You were so happy, in fact, that a few weeks later you presented him at show-and-tell in Mrs. Myer's kindergarten class. And Jimmy, last spring you bounded up Connecticut Avenue, bursting with pride and yelling at the top of your lungs, "I've got a library card. I can't believe I have my own library card!"—an important step toward growing up. These are just the beginnings of the memories that will shape your lives.

While clipping rose blossoms for my sisters' and my bouquets for the school May procession, my mother shared memories of *her* mother, Anna, an Italian immigrant and wonderful cook. Mom had transplanted and nurtured grandma's two climbing roses—a red and a white—and each spring they always reminded her of her youth. She was raised in the country and always decried the constraints of city life; she said that children should live free enough to enjoy some mischief—and we did, to her delight. And so my personal history began with stories of my grandmother as told by my mother on sunny mornings in May.

While my grandmother's story provided flavor, my mother provided the values while she worked as a homemaker. Raking leaves, refinishing furniture, or cleaning beans while relaxing on the back porch, she shared her own maxims:

- You can't understand another's views until you've walked in his shoes.

- Trust in the strength of your convictions.

- Don't complain unless you are willing to work toward a solution.

- It takes two to tango; the problems in a relationship are never totally one-sided.

The last was especially poignant. She raised my three sisters, my brother, and me essentially alone because my father suffered from alcoholism and mental illness. There were worries, yes, and there were scenes. And when she faced a crisis, she solved it, knowing that six lives were at stake. She was our mother, and she never saw her future as separate from ours. Isn't that a standard for all? Just like a gardener, the commitment must be for life.

Mothering today is different than in the 1960s. Today the opportunities that shape each mother's day abound. I chose a profession that allowed me to establish a home office. I wanted the flexibility to see my children's faces after school each day. I wanted them and their friends "under my feet"—maybe not daily but enough to have the decibel level raised after 3 p.m. With this arrangement, we have raised a dog, ducklings, and a hamster. We have dug for carrots and blown ladybugs off our fingers. We have weathered arguments, lost toys, and taken trips to the hospital.

And they have brought hilarity into the office. Baby Jimmy loved to ride the photocopier when its carriage moved across a document. A few years later he interrupted a meeting to show us how he cleverly zipped the hamster inside his fanny pack. Jodi has held my surveyor's rod on a project site so I could shoot elevations. Our time together has been interspersed with said and unsaid nothings and somethings—a shared fertility in which roots can thrive. Their presence intertwines my day so that I never will have to regret having "missed" their childhood.

What will mothering in the future be like? I hope Jodi chooses to find out. For her, the opportunities and the pressures will be greater. Many of the academic and professional glass ceilings will be gone. This will require more nuanced choices.

She will succeed easily in the business world, but at what cost? Will she understand that to mother—not just to birth—a child will require a delicate balance of her time and her own resources? Will she be in a profession that allows her to design her day; will it be integrated or split? Will she have the inner awareness and determination to demand an arrangement that meets her needs and the needs of her children? Will she be at peace with the awareness that "doing it all" is an impractical goal that will ultimately compromise her centeredness? For Jodi, I believe the answer is "yes." But what about future mothers who don't have those memories of time with their moms as a reference point or who live under difficult circumstances?

Today's divorce law and its enforcement often do not secure the resources necessary for a mother to continue her time at home with her children. With divorce, it is not unusual for middle-aged women to feel forced to shift from homemaker to wage earner to survive financially. The result is more precarious than in the past. For my mother, even with financial insecurities, her house was secure, she was assured good health insurance, and we went to safe, good schools. Unfortunately that picture has changed. The family home is often sold. "Latchkey children" spend after-school hours in empty houses. Gun-related violence is more common. Minimal health insurance is secured at great cost. And ultimately that precious time of mother and child together is lost.

My prayer for our future mothers is that we be mindful and protective of the securities necessary for women to mother and for children to grow. If we don't, then the easy transference of values and the rich creativity of our oral history will suffer as mothers, the gardeners of mankind, struggle for survival. And eventually the stories of ladybugs and grandma's roses will fade, and the standard by which we measure the quality of life will fall.

If we do provide security, then I predict that same value system will enhance the robustness of other aspects of the garden, such as the environment and community and the global village.

In summary, I am reminded of something I wrote years ago at a time I was deeply aware of the joy of raising my first child, made more poignant by the heartache of infertility. "She has given me so much. She has made me a mother with pictures, parent jargon, Halloween, Christmas. When I watch her now, it is with two sets of eyes. One set watches her as any mother would. The other set struggles to memorize perfectly the soft curves of her face, the unfaltering trust of her hand in mine, the wonder in her eyes as the world unfolds. For this gift, I am so thankful and wish that I could share." This memory-making must always be in our future.

*Martha Donnelly Paci, a landscape architect, and her husband Tom are the parents of Jodi and Jimmy.*

# Holy SpaghettiOs

## *Ellen Palmer Sands*

The birth of our children was also the birth of my prayer life. Growing up, I'd had an erratic religious education, so I wasn't sure where to begin. "Dear God," I'd pray hesitantly, late at night, rocking Amy, "please make her go to sleep."

Recognizing the inadequacy of this approach, I looked to the *Catechism of the Catholic Church,* where I found satisfying passages on what prayer is and isn't. "Prayer," it says, "cannot be reduced to the spontaneous outpouring of interior impulse,"(§2650). Well, with three young children, I have more "interior impulses" in a day than I know what to do with. So, seeking some structure, I turned to the comfort of traditional prayer.

I found an essay titled "Slowing Down the 'Our Father.'" It contends that we have so internalized this keystone of our faith that we no longer really hear its petitions. It's a good point, but the opposite can be argued as well. It isn't that I race through the "Our Father"; it takes me twenty-three seconds. I know because I have prayed it while microwaving SpaghettiOs. It gives new meaning to the directions "on High."

Prayer helps us step back and remember Christ's role in our lives. What better time to reflect on patience, love, and humor than when dealing with tired and hungry children, tired and hungry mothers.

Praying while pumping gas on Georgia Avenue also works well. Cars rush by, drivers inside convinced their errand or commute or soccer practice is crucial. And, for those twenty-three seconds, I am not a part of it. When I'm finished, the hubbub doesn't matter quite so much. I'm tranquil. Perhaps prayer relocates me—or perhaps it's simply that for those brief moments, the children are inside the car and I'm not.

Still, thinking this might be considered indiscriminate prayer, I went back to the *Catechism*. "His Spirit," it says, "is offered to us at all times in the events of *each day*" (§2659). In the words of St. John Chrysostom, "It is possible to offer fervent prayer while walking in public or strolling alone,...while buying or selling...or even while cooking" (§2743). I felt better about the SpaghettiO's.

Most often, "the events of each day" in which Christ offers us his spirit aren't momentous. They are small and mundane, like praying over the microwave or the gas pump. But strung together they are significant, particularly when we think about our children's lives. I offer three brief anecdotes from our family, one for each of our children, so they are equitably embarrassed.

- Nora, at about age three, was marching through the living room with a banner pole. "Look, Mom," she called. "I'm the Jesus guy. I'm Father D'Silva."

- Our nine-year-old, Bill, was fishing in Pennsylvania last summer. Not catching anything, he suggested,

"Why don't we just do this like the apostles and get a really big net?"

- Finally, on one of Amy's report cards last year, a teacher related how our daughter, then eleven, had welcomed a new girl to the class. Later the gym teacher told me how Amy had resolved a playground argument over choosing teams, matter-of-factly declaring that the left-out boy would be on her team and that it was time to start playing.

The thread in these stories, besides just bragging about my children, is that all of our children, at their own developmental level, absorb the lessons they learn at church each week and from us on a daily basis. Initially, like Nora at age three, they see only the rituals and the trappings. As they get older, like Bill last summer, the stories in the gospel become part of their frame of reference for interpreting situations. Finally, as the teen years approach, like Amy they apply these teachings in making decisions and choosing what kind of person they will become.

I now realize that my prayers for more patience, more love, or more good humor don't enable me to transform life's tedious, angry, or trying events. But they do transform *me* and how I react.

I have at best simplistic notions of where this all leads. Father D'Silva refers to heaven as "a big party." Well, I've been to some truly great parties. But I also know one of the secrets of a good party is knowing when to call it quits and go home. So the idea of a party for all eternity strikes me as hard to sustain and kind of exhausting.

I like to think, instead, that the answer to all of our prayers is right here. Heaven is here on earth, for mothers, for fathers, sisters, or brothers. It's how we live our lives, and it surrounds us every day.

***Ellen Palmer Sands,*** *an architect, is married to David; their children are Amy, Bill, and Nora.*

# A Gift from My Children

## Susan Mitchell

A while ago, *The Washington Post* published an article titled, "What Are Children For?" I was appalled by the casual thoughtlessness of the question. I wrote in response that we are all children of God and that, by dividing ourselves into separate age groups, separate countries, and separate faiths, we forget that no one of us has any more value than another. We also forget that our value comes from God and not from anything we do. This is a lesson no mother needs to be taught from the moment she first sets eyes on her child.

What I would like to address here is how motherhood—and particularly the sacraments my children have received—have helped me in *my* faith.

I am a cradle Catholic, as the term goes, and Catholic rituals such as the annual May crowning of Mary were important to me. I received Vatican II with gusto as a young teenager and remember singing at folk Masses, home Masses, outdoor Masses, everywhere imaginable. As a young adult, however, I began to drift away from the faith, not out of any conscious decision but because I just got caught up in the busyness of life.

My husband and I were married in the Catholic Church—St. Peter's on Capitol Hill. But it wasn't until my son Mitchell was baptized at a splendid candlelight Easter Vigil with a cast of thousands—and special effects of thunder and lightning as the priest said, "Let there be light"—that I began again to think seriously about my faith. We read Bible stories, taught prayers at home, and went to Mass occasionally. The baptism of my daughter, Catherine, again prompted a resurgence of faith. But again, the details of daily life with two young children took over.

This casual faith began to change during Mitchell's first communion year. I found that by having to explain the meaning and significance of the sacraments of reconciliation and Eucharist to both my son and my husband, who is Presbyterian, I began to yearn for them myself. At my son's first reconciliation, I went to confession for the first time since high school, and I'll never forget Father D'Silva's words of "Welcome back."

It was during Mitchell's first communion ceremony in 1990, in fact, during a song written by Carey Landry and Nancy Bourassa called "A Gift from Your Children," that I heard the words: "Here is our gift, a gift ever new. In giving to others we give unto you. A gift, a gift from your children, the gift, the gift of our love."

In hearing those words, I realized that it was through my son's faith that I was receiving my own back again. It wasn't I, as mother, giving my faith to him, but rather he by *his* faith and love who was giving it to me.

My daughter's first communion provided another dimension, one which showed the interconnectedness of motherhood stretching behind and before me. During the planning for her first Eucharist in 1993, my father had a stroke and was confined to home. Neither he nor my mother was going to be able to attend, and I was devastated. Suddenly, during the planning meeting, I had a thought: Why not do a home Mass? My parents' priest in Connecticut, who didn't know Catherine or me, readily agreed. We had twelve people in my parents' living room on my mother's seventieth birthday, and my daughter wore my communion dress and veil, which my mother lovingly had preserved. Each child did a reading, and the room was brimming with love and faith.

By these sacraments, I feel I have been called back to the church and to service within it. Motherhood has not been a one-way street in terms of faith. I have experienced my faith anew through my children.

*Susan Mitchell has a master's degree in pastoral studies and completed a clinical pastoral education program. She works as a certified Catholic chaplain at Montgomery Hospice in Rockville, Maryland. She and her husband Arthur Fraas are the parents of Arthur Mitchell Fraas and Catherine Fraas.*

# Mother Teresa's Prayer

## *Debbie Buckley*

I often think of the twists and turns my life takes and how it affects my personal journey closer to God. I marvel, really, at what I consider to be miracles in my everyday existence.

What a miracle to meet Jerry, a spiritual and devout Catholic, when I was in my mid-30s. A non-practicing Episcopalian, I began going to church with him every week, and it wasn't long before I found myself being moved more and more by the Mass. Shortly after our marriage, I joined the Roman Catholic Church. Our faith was a source of guidance and strength when, sadly, it seemed that children did not seem to be in God's plan for us.

Through more of life's twists and turns, I eventually found myself involved in northeast work with Mother Teresa's Missionaries of Charity, who run a residential facility called Gift of Peace for sick and dying homeless men and women on Otis Street in northeast Washington, D.C. The blessings I received through that work were immeasurable. Sister Delores, at that time the superior at Gift of Peace, knew of my and my husband's strong desire to have a family. She knew of our profound sadness at having lost several pregnancies. She had mentioned to me several times a prayer Mother Teresa had recommended to others who desired children and told me their prayers had been answered. I must admit, I listened, but, as they say, did not hear.

In the summer of 1987, Mother Teresa was visiting Washington, D.C. Sister Delores suggested that Jerry take off work (not easy for a Washington lawyer), and she would introduce us to Mother and tell her our story, and Mother would tell us a prayer to say so we would have a baby. Sister Delores had such a simple, child-like belief that this absolutely would happen. I had witnessed so many signs of God's love at Gift of Peace that I thought, at the very least, this prayer would make things clear to us.

We did meet Mother Teresa. She did, indeed, tell us a prayer to say. It simply goes: "Mary, Mother of Jesus, give us a baby."

We were to say the prayer many times a day—together, when we were not together, silently and aloud—and we would have a baby. I must say, I was 100 percent sure our prayer would be answered, but not 100 percent sure our definition of *baby* was the same as God's. I told Jerry that maybe our child as defined by God might not be what we expected. Perhaps his plan was for us to "parent" the grown residents of Gift of Peace, the poorest of the poor.

But Jerry and I faithfully said the prayer. And we both were confident that, in saying it, God would make clear what his idea of parenting was to be for us.

The next month—five years into our marriage, one month after meeting Mother Teresa, one month of constantly saying our prayer—our daughter Mary was conceived. She was born on May 31, the month of Our Lady, the Feast of the Visitation, 1988.

Why me? I ask this often. I continue to see miracles in my life—skeptics might say coincidences. Our twin girls were another miraculous gift, born May 1, 1991.

So I was on the blacktop here at Blessed Sacrament School several months ago, and Father D'Silva approached and asked whether I would speak to this group on Mother's Day. (Oh no, I thought, why me? And how clever of him to ask so far in advance that I couldn't possibly already have plans.) I must admit to waking in the middle of the night the last few months mulling over this moment. I thought of every angle of Mother's Day I could conjure up. What I began to realize was that something I initially viewed as a sort of penance became a gift, an opportunity in which I truly have grown spiritually. It became a personal retreat, and I have been greatly enriched by the experience. So once again, one of life's twists and turns has been enriching spiritually.

I thought about my own mother and her sacrifices in raising four children. How hard it must have been for her to work every day and yet always prepare a family dinner for us. Of course, I thought about the most perfect of mothers, Our Lady, how her example is always before us and how easy it is to get caught up in our busy world and not see her guiding us. I thought about Mother Teresa, her Missionaries of Charity and their many volunteers (both male and female), and how they are mothers in every sense of the word to the poorest of the poor, how by observing them we can broaden our definition of mothering. I thought, of course, about myself and the type of mother I am and the type of mother I wish I were and strive daily to be.

So if you see Father D'Silva approaching, resist the urge to bolt in the other direction.

*Debbie Buckley* *works part-time as a dental hygienist. She and her husband Jerry have three daughters: Mary, and twins, Anne and Gretta.*

# Mother's Been Carried Off by the Iroquois

*Donnamarie Mills*

Did all Catholics, certainly those of us over thirty-five, confuse the Blessed Virgin with their own mothers when they were young? Certainly I did. When I sang "On This Day, O Beautiful Mother," I thought of Mom. This confusion was exacerbated by the fact that Raphael's painting *Madonna of the Chair,* a replica of which always hung over our piano, did not look unlike my Italian-American mother, with the exception of the June Cleaver look-alike hairdo—on Mom, that is, not the Virgin, who wore her usual veil. The watchful brown eyes were particularly similar.

I don't know if you are familiar with this painting, but the eyes of the Blessed Mother seem to follow you around the room. My sister Marty found this effect to be spooky. She was convinced the portrait was beckoning her with its gaze to become a nun, rather like an Uncle-Sam-Wants-You poster. My sister, who did not want to become a nun, actually developed a small crisis about this. She had to be reassured by our mother and by our aunt, who was and is a nun, that one way you knew you truly had a vocation was that the thought did not scare you silly.

My sister eventually married and became a mother, as

did all three of the girls in our family of six siblings. But if anyone had asked us when we were little what we wanted to be when we grew up, we would have answered writer, or ballerina, or in one sister's case, a racehorse, but none of us would have said "a mother."

As children, we lived in New Hampshire on the edge of a wooded area. In those more casual days, children often were allowed outside until suppertime or when the streetlights came on. Consequently we had long hours to play in those woods, and the favorite game was pioneers. Being true children of Disney, we modeled ourselves on Davy Crockett or sometimes Francis Marion, the Swamp Fox. Inspired by real Indian massacres that occurred nearby some two hundred years ago, we often worked these into the plot. But one thing I remember keenly from those days: almost nobody ever wanted to play the mother. We got around this by pretending that Mother had been carried off by the Iroquois. That way nobody would be stuck back at the ranch, so to speak.

Obviously, from our vantage point as children, mothering did not seem like a very exciting job. Almost all of our mothers were at home fulltime. I am sure, however, that if pressed we would not have described our fathers' lives as very exciting either. They lacked that heroic dimension we craved.

I think what we failed to grasp was that our parents, all of whom had lived through the Depression and World War II, many as combatants, had had all the excitement they could ever want. To experience the slow rhythms and banalities of family life must have seemed to them, I think, a great privilege. And certainly they did radiate an energy, all those young families shoehorned into their little houses, full of life and promise. But when I was ten, I would not have described it that way. I tended to identify with lively heroes, often male. I loved the *We Were There* series, *On the Oregon Trail,* the Lincoln-Douglas debates, and when I could find them, the autobiographies of interesting women such as Sacagawea, Louisa May Alcott, and Harriet Tubman.

As a student in Catholic schools for six years, I also had access to *Lives of the Saints.* Whose lives could have been more fascinating than the Blackrobes, the missionaries, the apostles? There were heroic women saints as well, but many of them, such as St. Cecelia and St. Agnes, met a bad end, at least from my juvenile point of view, and certainly none of the biggies—Joan of Arc, Teresa of Avila, and Catherine of Siena—were mothers. In the panoply of saints, Mary herself had the monopoly on motherhood, but it seemed very presumptuous to identify with her.

Now that I am a mother, however, I think of her example a great deal. It is fair to say that as a child, I was ambivalent about motherhood. To be a mother was to be in the background, necessary perhaps, like oxygen, but not very interesting.

What I have learned since is that motherhood is anything but boring—far different than my ten-year-old brain could imagine, but hardly boring. In our household, dramas are being played out all the time. Still, the consolations of being a parent can be hard to explain to the uninitiated, though instantly clear to those of us who have joined "the motherhood," as one writer recently put it. You simply cannot know until you have them just how much you will love your children. Much of what makes motherhood compelling are the bonds of love and of hope and of faith, the sense that the family is a creation and that its possibilities are, literally, almost limitless.

But that's not what you think about during the 3 a.m. feeding. More than once when I was at Chevy Chase Supermarket—it always seemed to happen there, infant Tony drooling in a baby seat, four-year-old Portia running alongside throwing in groceries we didn't need, and three-year-old Philip literally on his leash—an older woman would come up to me and say, "Enjoy it, dear. These are the best years of your life." I would give her a long Carol-Burnett look. Say what? You mean from here it goes downhill?

I know now what these ladies, these mothers further along the journey than I was at that time, really were trying to tell me: that it all goes by very, very quickly. And then you are going to want it back.

What wouldn't you give years later to be able to hug them again as they were when they were only a year or two old? Just for half a minute?

This thought has been much in my mind these days because we just faced a milestone: our eighth grader was confirmed last week. We know from having been through it once before that this is the beginning of the long good-bye that is high school. As parents, we have reached the time to try—as it says in the old Joni Mitchell song—to slow down the circles. But how is that accomplished?

Sometimes I think the sheer busyness of our lives contributes to that fast-forward feeling. In fact, around here, busyness seems to have become a status symbol. This is where I find Catholicism with its Sunday obligations, its sacraments, and its rituals so indispensable. As you observe them, you are forced to slow down, to reflect. As the years go by, these events become markers. So much in between is forgotten. But at Christmas, funerals, first communions, weddings, and weekly Mass, we come together as families and as part of the family of God. For me, family life without these things is hard to imagine. They remind us, if I may borrow another's words, "of the wisdom and vast joy that underlies the tattered blanket of our lives."*

But as with all things that include children, this attempt to impose order can be pretty disorderly. Our household was not a pretty sight a half hour before we all were due to arrive at church for confirmation. And I can't think of a Mass in recent memory when I haven't had to hiss, "Use a Kleenex," to one of my children.

I have a shorthand prayer I recite at such times: "Lord, whose heart is larger than our hearts, please make up the difference." This is shorthand for a variation on the following: We are trying; we can't make it; we know how we would like it to be, how it should be. Please make it a more perfect offering, or something like that. Amen.

---

*Brian Doyle, "Altar Boy," *The American Scholar,* Spring 1997.

The other day I was emptying out a vase. It was filled with bits of debris—paper clips, buttons, pennies—probably thrown in there just to get them out of sight. At the bottom were several little pieces of paper, all wadded up. Unfolding them, I found short messages in my children's handwriting of several years ago.

On the first one was scrawled, "Be nicer to Tony." The second one said—and here was my clue—"Give up being mean to Tony." The third one, in the largest hardest-to-read handwriting, said, "Stop tattling on Portia and Philip." I then recalled an Ash Wednesday several years ago when the youngest three had agreed to write down what they were giving up for Lent and put the papers into the vase to be retrieved on Easter. Apparently in the middle of finding Easter baskets, we had forgotten to go back and reread these Lenten promises.

I never did find out if Tony had noticed a new benevolence on the part of his older brother and sister, who had apparently given up torturing him for the space of a few weeks, perhaps only a few days. I can only hope that here again, the Lord, whose heart is larger than our hearts, made up the difference.

*Donnamarie Mills, a part-time writer and editor specializing in energy issues, and her husband Mark are the parents of four children: Brendan, Portia, Philip, and Anthony.*

# I Believe

*Emily Collins*

I believe.
I believe in God.
I believe in my family.
I believe in home-cooked meals
whenever possible. However,
I also believe
in hoagies, hot dogs, Boston Chicken,
and pizza with pepperoni.
That you can have
a good meal
without cloth napkins,
crystal glasses,
and trying to figure out a French menu.

I believe in hard decisions
and hard work.
That people who take
the easy way out
eventually pay
the hard way.
I believe in free speech,
free enterprise,
and freeways.

That your freedom ends
when it enslaves mine.

I believe sometimes
one and one
make three.
That it's better to be
judged by twelve
than carried by six.

I believe in Jesus,
John, Paul,
George, and Ringo.

I believe in movies
that make you laugh,
music that makes you cry,
and books that make you strong.
That people who think
they know all the answers
don't even know the question.

I believe in action,
acts of kindness,
acts of courage.

I believe it is possible
to gain notoriety
without doing something wrong
and then writing a book about it.

I believe in life.
Life at conception.
Life after birth.
Life in the hereafter.
I believe that it is
fragile, sacred, and singular.

I believe in motherhood.
I believe that bringing
a child into the world
is just the beginning.
That teaching a child
to grow, learn, love,
and survive
is a mother's most important work.

I believe in Mary,
the mother of God.

I believe in Mother Teresa
and her exemplary life.

I believe in my own
mother, my mother-in-law,
mothers of my children's friends,
all of the mothers
who have taught me
the values and virtues
that are passed along
through the generations.

I believe in my husband,
whose love, strength,
and sense of humor
have given our family
the confidence to succeed.

I believe in my children.
They have given me more
than they will ever realize.

I believe in true friends,
trusting families,
and the tradition of our faith.

I am Emily Collins and
I believe.

*Emily Collins and her husband Pat have raised three children: Patrick, Michael, and Salley.*

# Surprise!
# Moms Aren't Perfect

*Marie Barry*

Last Mother's Day, in our church parking lot, a long-time friend, a father, announced that his kids should send *him* a Mother's Day card. I agreed wholeheartedly. He was the person who nurtured and was always there for his children.

Someone once gave a joking definition of a mother as "the one who attends," meaning the one who is present at innumerable events. But really that is not such a bad definition. A mother is someone who attends to and is emotionally bonded with a child. When the birth mother (or father) cannot do that, the role can be and is being filled everyday by grandparents, other family members, adoptive and foster parents, teachers, religious, coaches. I honor them for their role in mothering and for their faithfulness to the Gospel call—to Jesus' message—to care for one another.

When I was a young mother, I felt tentative about my mothering capabilities; after my fourth was born, I thought I was beginning to get the hang of it. In fact, I got more than a bit self-righteous, taking my way of doing things as the right and possibly only way to raise children.

As my children tiptoed or roared through their teen years, depending on their personalities, and emerged into their twenties, I was right back where I started as a mother—

tentative, confused. I saw other children who were raised very differently from mine and who turned out fine. I didn't have the answers anymore.

My three girls confronted me with things from the past. (Note: Daughters tend to be harder on mothers than sons are.) They asked: "Why did you do that? How could you have said that?" For my part, I was equally appalled: Why *did* I do that? How *could* I have said that? I asked for their forgiveness and understanding. After all, I had not consciously set out to do them wrong. At the time, I thought what I did was right, or at least understandable. But then gradually I realized that their questioning of me was an important part of their own growing up, of their accepting their own imperfections.

I am not and was never a perfect mother. They also will not be perfect mothers, and that's all right. We're human; we make mistakes. It's part of the human condition. As Henri Nouwen so beautifully put it: "Jesus wants us to receive the love he offers....The great temptation is to use our many failures to convince ourselves that we are really not worth being loved."*

It is important for me to accept God's forgiveness for my failings, not only to help myself but to show my children the way. Since there is no such thing as guaranteed results in parenting, we do the best we can, with what we have, and leave the rest in God's hands.

Now the world and society are rapidly changing. America is becoming much more of a multiracial society.

---

*Quoted in *Returning: God's Love Calls Us Home,* edited by James E. Adams (St. Louis, MO: Creative Communications, 1989), 4.

Tiger Woods proudly proclaims himself a "Cablinasian" in recognition of all his ethnic strains: Caucasian, Black, Native American, and Asian. My daughter Deirdre's husband, Ron, is African American, so our grandsons, three-year-old Andrew and two-week-old Liam, could be called Afro-Celts. They are mirrors of the future; the future is here and now. I wish for them a world free of prejudice, free of violence and hate, free of poverty and immigrant-bashing.

Regardless of the real world, we know that God calls each of us to do good. We believe that each person is made in the image and likeness of God. Our dignity comes from God—not from the place we live, the parents we have, our ethnic group—but from God who knew us in the womb and holds us in the palm of his hand. How could we ever be mean or unfair to one of his created ones? As the reading from the first letter of John says: "Beloved, since God loved us so much, we also ought to love one another"(1 John 4:11).

We are on a pilgrimage. Each and every day is precious. Each and every day moves us closer to our ordained end: union with God in heaven. Each and every day is another chance to show our love for one another here on earth. So let us rejoice and be glad.

*Marie Barry, formerly an employee of the Archdiocese of Washington, gives talks and workshops on Catholic social teaching to dioceses and parishes nationally. She also helps them organize for advocacy. She and her husband Paul have four adult children—Deirdre Barry Allen, Maura, Gretchen, and Matthew Barry—and three grandchildren.*

# My Guardian Dear

*Josie Olsvig Moorman*

Seventeen months ago, God bestowed a special blessing on my husband Tom and me. Her name is Allison Ingrid. She is a clever, strong-willed child, and I now realize I'm being paid back for every gray hair I ever gave my parents.

Tom and I are a bit older than other first-time parents. We married in 1994 after dating for a brief time in the late 1970s in our hometown of Dayton, Ohio. For a variety of reasons, we went our separate ways for about thirteen years before meeting up again in 1993. I went through thirty-nine years of waiting and dreaming about having a child before I had Allison. It has only served to make parenthood even more special for us.

For the first year of Allison's life, I was able to stay home with her. Then, late last summer, I got a call inviting me to interview for a job that would draw on my experience as a social worker and as a prosecuting attorney specializing in child-abuse and sex-offense cases. Ultimately, I was offered the job—director of a nonprofit organization called "Lawyers for Children." It seemed wonderful, but it meant I had to leave "my little pumpkin."

I don't know who cried more when Allison entered daycare, but we adjusted. Her daycare is in the building behind me. I can get to her in two minutes if I want.

As a parent, I have come to better understand God's unconditional love. Through colic, dirty diapers, sleepless nights, and endless days of colds and runny noses, I have loved my daughter, as God loves each one of us. I have savored those moments when I rock her to sleep in my arms and just stare at her and caress her head. I draw upon these moments when she refuses to go to sleep, or when she throws the TV remote control in the trash, or pulls all the Kleenex out of the box and watches each tissue float to the floor like a snowflake.

Recently, *Newsweek* published an issue on early-childhood development and the importance of good care and stimulation in the first year of life. This only supports what we mothers have known for a long time: the role of a mother is vital in the life of a child.

We all need to appreciate the importance of mothers in a child's life, along with the frustrations and difficulties that mothers face every day, all day. Lend support to a mom whenever you can. They need it. Allow mom to have a break now and then. Offer to watch the kids for a while for your sister, your friend, your neighbor or any mother you might know.

Unfortunately both of my parents are deceased, as are a great many members of my extended family. I have only one sibling, and she has been an Israeli resident since 1980. Fortunately I managed to marry into the large and boisterous Moorman clan. Tom is one of six children. My daughter is grandchild number fifteen. It has been great receiving this wonderful and warm extended family, and I think a child brings a couple and the extended family closer together.

The death of my parents and many other relatives has taught me to use my days wisely. My sister-in-law, Peg, often says, "Love one another. Life is too short not to appreciate your time together."

My father died several years before my mother did. A struggling single parent, my mother worked as a sales clerk in a department store in Ohio. She never missed a day of work unless she was in the hospital. She was not a perfect parent, but she did the best she could. Now I realize how hard it was for her.

As an adult, I was able to spend a great deal of time with my mother. She was able to see me graduate from law school. She used to love to threaten people with, "My daughter, she's a prosecutor."

I was able to take care of my mother in her final years, seeing her through heart by-pass surgery and then the lung cancer that ultimately killed her. People have differing opinions about having a parent move in with you. But I did it and am glad I did. I used to tell people that my mother had cared for me and changed my dirty diapers, and now it was my turn to care for her.

Being a parent has opened my eyes in new ways to God's presence. My spirituality has deepened. I have come to realize that God's guiding hand is always with me and that he employs his angels to assist him in his work.

We think that Allison's godfather, Jim, has become one of her guardian angels. Jim married Tom's sister Peg, whom

I went to college with, and they are my daughter's godparents. Unfortunately Jim was diagnosed with brain cancer in October 1996 and passed away seven weeks later.

In the first six months after his death, I think that Allison has seen Jim on at least three occasions. I cannot see him. But Allison appears to be interacting with someone. She has never identified him by name, but one time she pointed toward a place where she appeared to be focusing on someone and said, "Birdie." We have wondered whether she sees Jim with angel's wings.

Allison and I had our first angelic experience when she was about five months old. I had taken her grocery shopping and was starting to put away the groceries. Allison was in her "bouncer seat" on our family room floor at the end of our galley kitchen. I purchased some fresh flowers that day and climbed up on a chair to retrieve a crystal vase from the top of our kitchen cabinets. Allison was below me, a few feet to my left. As I grabbed this heavy vase, I accidentally dropped it.

It started to fall toward my daughter, first hitting a candle in a glass jar and then suddenly going the other direction and landing twelve to fifteen feet away at the other end of the kitchen. It was like seeing a tip-off at a basketball game. This all happened very quickly, and my first thought was, "Isn't that odd how that landed?"

I immediately got down from my chair to check on my daughter. I thought she must have some glass splinters on her. There were glass splinters and white powder near her, but nothing on her. Ninety-five percent of the glass was quite a distance away at the far end of our kitchen. The floor was of very dark wood, and there was a clear circle, or line of demarcation, surrounding her. The white powder and bits of glass were a stark contrast with the dark wood. It looked like a bubble or shield had been over her, protecting her. There were splinters and small bits of broken glass about ten inches from her feet and also a couple of feet beyond her, but absolutely nothing was on her.

Seeing this, it dawned on me that someone else was in that room with us. I just thought to myself, "I believe! I believe!" I cried for an hour after that.

Interestingly, when I tell this story to other parents, they often respond quite casually, "Oh, we have had several experiences like that."

I guess this is just something that goes with parenthood: diaper rash, ear infections, and angelic experiences.

*Josie Olsvig Moorman is an attorney and clinical social worker. She and her husband Tom are the parents of Allison Ingrid.*

# The Philosophy of "Why Not?"

*Terry Kobane*

A short ten years ago, I was single, just passing time working, playing, and hanging out with my dog. Motherhood was for my friends, my sister, and all those other people. I was content. I was happy. I had spare time, lots of it. I knitted. I read. I went to the movies.

Then one day, on May 10, 1990, I met Tim Hirt. He came to my door for a blind date, a lunch date. He tried to talk me out of a piece of the fried chicken I had just made for a picnic later that day. He quickly learned that I say "no" several times before I say "yes," and I quickly learned that he just keeps on asking.

Love struck us hard. Much to my family's astonishment, I was forming a relationship with a divorced man who was raising three small children by himself. I have a dear friend who says I'm one of those people who subscribes to the philosophy of "why not?"

We quickly added two beautiful girls to Tim's three young children. It was only recently that my gynecologist laughed and confided that she and her nurses were taking bets on when I would wake up and say, "My goodness, what have I done having all these kids?"

We joined Blessed Sacrament Parish in 1994. Not knowing the rules, I pushed that double stroller right up the aisle of the Mass held in the gym and began the long journey of trying to get my kids to behave like adults in church.

It took me a long time to figure out how to make it through Mass without feeling like a warden. I would come out exhausted. Things have gotten better. I've learned to put an adult between the kids. And I've also learned to go to church by myself on Wednesdays.

I'd like to share part of my journey into motherhood. It's been one of learning and gratitude. Each of my children brings a special lesson or gift to me. You could not have convinced me of this in the first few years of motherhood. I still hung on to the delusion that I was the leader. In fact, we used to joke that the kids should address me as "Mommy Dearest, Queen of the Universe, Ruler of the World." I've given up thinking that I hold all the answers.

My oldest daughter Christy has taught me patience and tolerance. After years of trying to force my will upon her, I was struck with the notion that it had to be up to her to forge her own way and that my role should be only to support, encourage, and applaud her successes. This was very hard to swallow. I found it difficult to accept that she had rejected my way of thinking. After several years of getting on each other's nerves, we now enjoy the best relationship we ever have had. I pray every night for her happiness. For this I am grateful.

My son TJ has taught me the magic of unconditional love. He and I struggled for years. Again, I was busy pursuing my course for him in spite of repeated efforts on his part to do things his way. We have since drawn a truce and now have the utmost respect for each other.

I'll always remember when TJ was six and we pulled up to a 7-Eleven convenience shop after dark one evening. There were some menacing young men hanging out in front. I told this six-year-old that I didn't like the looks of them, and he replied, with all honesty, "Don't worry, Mom, I'll take care of you." For his devotion and loyalty, I am grateful.

My son Michael at an early age openly shared his genuine and enthusiastic view of God with us. Little did I know just what a good job Blessed Sacrament School was doing until one day, I said in front of him, "Oh, my God." Michael quickly looked up at me with those beautiful blue eyes and gently told me that he learned in school that we are only to use God's name in prayer. He's a kind and gentle boy. I am grateful to be his mother.

Now on to Mackenzie, my firstborn. Well, you can imagine the spotlight on this child. A forty-year-old woman having her first child—there ought to be laws against that. Yes, I did stand by her crib and watch her breathe—every night, several times a night. I know I'm not alone in having done that. That's a definite mother thing. I've also watched her begin to look like me, be bossy like me, take everything too seriously like me, and worry about her schoolwork. That's my kind of kid! We call her the substitute mom. She's taught me to let go of my fears, those fears that life will not be perfect for my children. I still watch her too closely; I probably always will. I'm grateful for her in my life each day.

And last, but not least, there's Kylie. Kylie teaches me to stop and smell the roses. She is blessed with a light and cheerful outlook on life. She's the one who had trouble pronouncing her *r*'s when she was younger. On one particular day, she looked me in the eye, put her hands on both sides of my face, and said, "Mom, you're a bootiful, bootiful wose." She's taught me to strive to be in the moment. She lives in the moment. I'm grateful for her cheery presence in my life.

I love being a mother.

My babysitter had a baby a couple of weeks ago. All of her family is in the Czech Republic. She and I often would hang out in my kitchen and talk. She misses her mother. I tried to tell her that she would feel very special about her new baby. I tried to tell her that these already very strong feelings only would get stronger and stronger. I told her to get ready; her life would never be the same. I told her to trust God and the delivery room nurses, and she would be taken care of. I visited her last week. Her baby is beautiful, and she loves being a Mom. Imagine that!

*Terry Kobane, wife of Tim Hirt, was also known as mother of the "red-haired children": Christy, Timothy Jr., aka TJ, Michael, Mackenzie, and Kylie. Nine months after giving this speech, Terry was diagnosed with a melanoma and died July 1, 2001, at age forty-nine.*

# And the Wisdom to Know the Difference

*Erika Ziebarth Jones*

On my confirmation day, nearly thirty years ago, my mother and father gave me a medal, a gold rectangle on a gold chain. On one side was a dove, the symbol of the Holy Spirit. On the reverse was an engraved prayer:

"God, grant me the serenity to accept the things I cannot change, the courage to change the things I can, and the wisdom to know the difference."*

That little prayer has meant a lot to me over the years. Although the medal itself is long lost, the prayer is forever imprinted in my memory. I remember it whenever I confront a decision involving change. It reminds me that some things are better left alone, and some things need to be changed.

This little prayer offers important lessons for mothers and fathers about some of the most difficult tasks of modern parenting. How much freedom do we allow our children to make their own decisions? When do we step in to veto their decisions? Where do we get the "wisdom to know the difference"?

The first lesson of the little prayer is sometimes to leave well enough alone. In our children's lives, this means there

---

*The Serenity Prayer. Its authorship is unknown but is often attributed to theologian Reinhold Niebuhr.

are times we should allow them to make their own decisions, letting them gain self-confidence when their decisions are good ones, and letting them learn from their mistakes when their decisions turn out less than perfect. It is hard not to step in and prevent our children from making mistakes, whether we spot errors in their homework, or in their choice of an after-school activity, or sometimes, in their choice of friends. We want their lives to be perfect. Yet it is important that we refrain from second-guessing their decisions so that our fledglings can learn to fly by their own wings.

Our children are with us such a short time. We can give them the ability and self-confidence to fly on their own wings only by allowing them the freedom to make their own decisions—even if they are mistakes—and to live by the consequences. The little prayer recognizes that it takes a special gift—serenity—to accept things as they are and resist the temptation to rush in and make things better.

On the other hand, the little prayer also recognizes that some things need to be changed. In the lives of our children, there are some circumstances in which we need to intervene, to overrule our children's decisions. The prayer reminds us that it is hard to intervene, something requiring courage. Every mother—and everyone else—can agree that it takes courage to tell a child that he or she cannot do something that "everyone else" is allowed to do. It takes courage to say, "No, you are not going to that party because you were not invited"; or, "No, you are not wearing torn jeans to your grandmother's house"; or, "No, you are not going out with that group, because we do not know everyone who is part of the group, and we do not like the ones we know."

Our children need limits, clearly articulated and consistently enforced. They need us to step in and enforce the rules to protect them when their unfettered decisions would expose them to harm.

But how do we know the difference between the times we should butt in and butt out? Exactly where do we get the "wisdom to know the difference"?

In our faith tradition, the "wisdom to know the difference" comes through the Holy Spirit. I believe that, but it is not an entirely satisfactory answer. The Holy Spirit does not have an 800 number, a Post Office box, or a reference guide at Borders.

As children ourselves, we learn "the wisdom to know the difference" from our own mothers. Our mothers allowed us certain freedoms and set certain rules. Whether we think they struck the right balance—or whether we think the balance should have been struck in a different place—mothers have had the strongest influence on us. Our mothers-in-law also have a strong influence if we choose to allow them as a source of wisdom. After all, they raised the men we married. They have good ideas, if we will welcome them into our lives.

Yet we need even more sources of this kind of wisdom. I believe that the Holy Spirit grants us this wisdom from each other—from the people here in this parish and the community at large. One of the best sources of wisdom I have found is the annual "parent peer group" meeting sponsored by our daughter's school. Most schools sponsor similar meetings, in which parents gather and talk about issues related to children of the same age. Inevitably some thorny situations arise that are addressed by a parent with an older child who went through the same issue a few years earlier.

This kind of sharing of experiences is the Holy Spirit working through each of us to give wisdom. And so we need to be open to these opportunities for shared wisdom and to be willing to share our own experiences when it is our turn.

One last thought: I expect that my mother does not remember giving me that particular medal with that particular prayer for my confirmation gift. My mother probably has no idea that this prayer—this gift from her—has been so influential in my life. And this observation itself suggests an important insight. We do not control—and cannot choose—what our children will elect to remember from their childhood. This thought presents us with a tremendous challenge. We must live each day and spend each moment as if it were the one moment—and maybe the last moment—that will live in our children's memories.

*Erika Ziebarth Jones is a partner in the Washington, D.C., office of the Chicago-based law firm Mayer, Brown, Rowe & Maw. She and her husband Gregory have one daughter, Katherine.*

# Final Lessons

## *Lorraine Kucik*

Some years ago, while I was studying theology at Trinity College, a professor asked, "If you were to choose three words to describe yourself, what would they be?" After some thought, I replied, "Christian, mother, and friend." Indeed, these words also describe my own mother, Anna Sincavage, and her life. In her quiet and unobtrusive way, she was my greatest teacher and role model.

I say quiet because she was not one to lecture or persuade with words. She was simply there: baking, gardening, or knitting an afghan to give as a gift. She climbed up and down the steep mountain of her Pennsylvania coal-mining town from her home on high to go down to Mass, to the store, or to visit a friend. Totally devoted to our large family, if something had to be done, she did it. If someone needed help, she was there. Although she undoubtedly suffered uncertainty and despair, as we all do, it rarely peeked through.

Even in the three years after a stroke crippled her at age eighty-six and stole her ability to speak and even to swallow, my mother was an inspiration to me. Her total unquestioning acceptance of God's will turned her time of suffering into one of Christian joy for those near her.

One of the oldest of eleven children, Anna grew up in the fold of a mountain in Plymouth, Pennsylvania, where my grandparents had migrated from Lithuania. She left school early, as many did at that time, to help support the family. And when her mother died at an early age, leaving behind youngsters as small as age five, my mom at age twenty-four helped in raising the smaller children.

I was born into that big family home atop a mountain incline where my mother lived most of her life. It was filled with aunts and uncles and friends, and I remember those days as among the happiest in my life. The times were marked by a reliance on family and friends as the immigrant families worked to gain a foothold in this country. It was good soil in which the Christian ethic of selflessness and helpfulness took root. Life, even social life, was centered on the church.

My mother's prayer life was important to her, though she was not boastful in ways of piety. In subtle ways, we always knew that Mother kept a direct line to our Lord.

As our family grew and left for distant cities, and after my dad's death, Mother and her sister remained at the homestead in Pennsylvania. I moved to Washington, D.C., but my family would visit her home many times a year in our workhorse of a station wagon, which my children dubbed "The Sunshine Cruiser." My mom would always poke her head out the front door as she saw the car pull up. She enjoyed seeing the house full of children and noise again. Bursting into her immaculately kept home, we'd be hit by the aroma of our favorite foods. The dining room table would be set in readiness.

After our meal, when the children had finished telling her their stories and settled in to play, she and I would catch up on each other's lives, and she would settle my fears and anxieties with her easy manner and impeccable advice. I would always leave feeling unburdened and refreshed, and months later, when the strain of young motherhood was again upon me, I would be back to visit, aglow as I saw her head peek out from the door.

Mother's pride in her twelve grandchildren and her great grandchildren (now numbering twenty-five) was constant. Baptisms, first communions, confirmations, graduations, and weddings filled her calendar. Often she traveled great distances, not wanting to miss any. When my son Matthew played football at Gettysburg College, she was his best cheerleader. She rarely missed a game.

Looking back at her life, it isn't her words so much as her mere presence that heartened me. She embodied a graceful morality and strength that attracted and instructed without effort. A great faith and dignity exhibited itself in her simple and often passive ways. Most importantly, she was always there.

It is no wonder then that when my mom suffered her stroke in late 1993, our decision to refuse the nursing-home option and instead to care for her at my brother's house in Pennsylvania was unanimous. With the help of my brother, Joe, and daily professional nursing care, I was the one most able to be her primary caregiver. My children were grown, and with their encouragement, I left my job, my theology studies, and my Washington house for three years to be with my mom in Pennsylvania.

Though she was bedridden and unable to speak all but

a few occasional words, her expressive eyes and unforgettable smile were always there in those final years. Her happiest times were when her family and especially her grandchildren came to visit. She was especially pleased when a newborn great grandchild was placed on her bed. Her room was often the stage for the latest dance step, play practice, or art class. She enjoyed visits from her many friends.

The measurement of love for one's mother could not surpass that of my dear younger sister Dorothy, who was in the final stage of cancer at that time. Up to the month before my sister died (two years before mom), in great discomfort from bone cancer and chemotherapy, she and her husband would make the long three-hour drive from Delaware to visit with Mother. Our times together resembled those of the past, happy and joyful, with my mom, my sister, and me miraculously enjoying times together again.

My mom and my sister suffered in an indescribable joy, always remembering that God was with them. In their illnesses, I believe, they were doing the work of our Lord. The nurses, who grew to love my mom over those three years, often expressed regret at not knowing Anna in her best years.

I will remember those years caring for Mother as one of the best times of my life. Alone much of the time, and with Mother unable to speak, I experienced a silent retreat in which I discovered the incredible power of prayer. I prayed that I, Mother, our family, and everyone involved in the suffering would be able to accept God's will, to truly profess: "Thy will be done." And he answered. The Lord is so near to us; so often we just don't realize it.

**Lorraine Kucik,** *the parish secretary at the Shrine of the Most Blessed Sacrament, has raised five children, mostly as a single parent. She is the mother of Teresa, George, Scott, Janine, and Matthew, and has eleven grandchildren.*

# A Job for King Solomon

*Ann O'Regan Keary*

When Father D'Silva asked me to speak at a Mother's Day Mass, I was reluctant. I told him I didn't like to speak in public, a fact that seemed to surprise him because he knew that my job requires me to speak in public all day long, every day. Ultimately I agreed because my children and husband really urged me to and because I always try to say "yes" to our children's requests whenever I can—so that I can continue to say "no" to the question I dread most, which they ask at least once a week: "Mom, can we get a dog?"

I also agreed to speak because, on some levels, my experience is worth talking about—not because, like so many women my age, I have a career and a family—but because in the last couple of years, I also have had a chance to do a lot of thinking about mothers and motherhood as a result of my work. I am a judge on the Superior Court of the District of Columbia, appointed by the president in 1992. At the time of my appointment, I had been juggling a legal career with motherhood for eleven years.

Many of my friends and fellow lawyers considered my judgeship a supreme achievement, the ultimate goal of many legal careers. My own view is that the crowning achievement of my life is my family—the three wonderful children with whom we have been blessed, and my wonderful husband,

213

Tom, who also juggles his legal career with family responsibilities and has been enormously supportive of my career. Our children play a crucial role in our lives, inspiring me to some of my greatest accomplishments at work. And they always help maintain my sense of humor and perspective, which is no small challenge in some of the emotionally draining assignments in the courthouse.

For the last couple of years, I have presided in numerous challenging cases of child neglect and abuse in which I, as judge, must choose whether a child should be reunited with a mother, placed outside the family, or adopted.

At a time when the media frequently tell us of the hopelessly fractured and broken nature of the family in some of the poorest segments of our community, I often am impressed by the positive images of mothering and caring I see in some of my cases. At times I have been quite moved by the selfless maternal instincts of some of the mothers, particularly in view of the tremendous obstacles some of them face, including drug addiction, a history of childhood abuse, or simply the hopelessness of poverty and under-education. For many of these young mothers, their child is the only positive and hopeful thing they can cling to, and it is clear that the greatest threat to such a young mother's well-being is the loss of that child.

In one shining moment of self-sacrifice, a young mother stood before me and tearfully agreed to allow her child to be adopted by the foster parent who had given the toddler a stable and loving home since birth. The birth mother had previously neglected the child but maintained an intense desire to be reunited. Despite that desire, she decided to leave her child with the foster mother with whom the child had bonded over the two-and-a-half years of her young life. The birth mother decided this was truly in her child's best interest, given her own continuing struggle with drugs.

This act of selflessness—putting aside personal wants because something else is better for her baby—is the ultimate definition of *motherhood*.

Being a mother myself for many years gives me a common bond with the women whose cases come before me, helping me appreciate their feelings and actions more fully and helping prepare me for the difficult decisions I must make over their and their children's lives.

My own mothering experience also helps me appreciate heroic stories of love in the cases of foster parents seeking to adopt their foster children. Recently I was impressed with a wonderful foster mother who sought to adopt the child who had been in her care since shortly after the child's birth and abandonment. She had to contend with whether the child's maternal relatives, who were unknown to the youngster, would have priority in adopting the child because of their biological connection. The commitment and intense love the foster mother showed surely couldn't have been exceeded even by a biological bond, and she ultimately won the adoption.

Being a mother also helps me empathize with the children—society's most vulnerable individuals—and makes me aggressively protective of their welfare. When I talk to children individually in neglect cases, I am amazed by the poor self-esteem some exhibit. In my own parenting experience, I now am even more careful to identify and praise the positive aspects of each child.

Maternal, nurturing behavior certainly is not limited to persons who are actually mothers. One of the most impressive examples of mothering I've seen involved two older single women who were active in their church in Anacostia, a poor section of Washington, D.C. They played a significant role in mothering a troubled and neglected teenage brother and sister who had no involved parents or other family. These women learned of the children's needs through their church and took these challenging teenagers into their own homes, although they barely had enough space for themselves and very little money. Yet they lovingly gave the guidance and nurturing that these youngsters desperately needed.

I also have been impressed with many men who are mentors for troubled or neglected young males through a program of Court Appointed Special Advocates. These young men often play remarkably nurturing and loving roles in the lives of our most troubled youths and demonstrate that mothering knows no gender bounds. Indeed, our daily lives are vastly enriched by the caring and loving qualities we identify as maternal as practiced by everyone in the community.

In closing, I hope I can always remember the wise parenting advice that complimenting children on their good behavior is probably more important than correcting their bad behavior. Positive encouragement of their best qualities, through praise for their actions, not only enhances their self-esteem but is an important factor in personal growth and maturity. I will continue to search for ways to reward my children for their impressive qualities and behavior, but I want them to understand, we're still not getting a dog.

*Ann O'Regan Keary, a D.C. Superior Court judge, and her husband Thomas have three children: Christopher, and twins James and Elizabeth, and still no dog.*